M 1 CHIP MACBOOK AIR USER GUIDE

THE ULTIMATE BEGINNER'S MANUAL TO USING THE LATEST M 1 CHIP MACBOOK AIR WITH TIPS AND TRICKS

BY

FELIX O. COLLINS

Contents

INTRODUCTION

Apple has updated the MacBook Air system with its new M1 chip in November 2020, the first Arm-based Apple chip designed. The M1 chip replaced the previous Intel chip and brought significant improvements in speed and efficiency.

The M1 chip is Apple's first Apple-system-on-chip chip, with an 8-core CPU, four high-performance cores and four high-performance cores, and an integrated GPU (up to eight cores). The CPU's CPU speed is three times faster than the previous generation model, while the GPU is five times faster.

The loading of the machine is nine times faster, so the MacBook Air speeds up ML-based features such as face recognition and object detection. With the help of the M1 chip, thanks to the new storage controller, SSD performance can be increased up to 2 times, while MacBook Air can be upgraded up to the last 2TB.

The maximum RAM capacity is 16GB and is integrated directly into the M1 chip to achieve integrated memory buildup, thus improving performance and efficiency. The battery life of the MacBook Air has been greatly improved, with up to 15 hours of web browsing and up to 18 hours of video playback.

Many changes to the MacBook Air are internal, not external. The MacBook Air does not have major construction updates and continues to use the pointed aluminum body, with a 13-inch Retina display, small bezels, and a large Force Touch Trackpad. The MacBook Air comes in a range of gray, silver, and gold.

The 13-inch display has a resolution of 2560x1600, similar to the previous model, but this year's new feature is supported by a wide-screen P3 screen, which can provide visible colors. It offers True Tone, which can match the white balance of the screen with existing light to give it a more natural viewing experience, and supports up to 400 light notes.

Apple's M1 MacBook Air is equipped with a 720p FaceTime HD camera, similar to the previous model, but Apple claims that the M1 has improved image quality by reducing better audio, more dynamic range, and other features.

Like the previous model, the M1 MacBook Air has a magic keyboard with a sophisticated scissor system, more reliable than the previous butterfly method, and can provide up to 1mm key movement to provide a stable key feeling.

The keyboard is well organized, and the operating keys now include "Do Not Disturb", set searches and call options, and a new emoji Fn key. You can use a Touch ID fingerprint sensor instead of a password to unlock your Mac, purchase, etc., and Touch ID is protected by Secure Enclave.

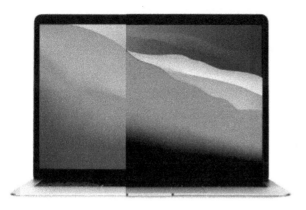

MacBook Air has two Thunderbolt 3 / USB 4 ports. These ports support 6K external displays and can be used with WiFi 6 or 802.11ax and Bluetooth 5.0. There are stereo speakers that support wide stereo, three microphone arrays, and a 3.5 mm headphone jack.

Features of M1 MacBook Air

Design

Compared to previous models, the M1 MacBook Air has no external design changes. It continues to be made with Apple's aluminum alloy, which uses 100% recycled aluminum and comes in two colors: silver, gray space, and gold.

The MacBook Air features a cone shape, which goes into the front of the metal. The thickest part of the MacBook Air is 0.63 inches and the thinner part is 0.16 inches. It is slightly stronger than the 2019 MacBook Pro, with its 0.61-inch thick area.

In size, the MacBook Air is 11.97 inches long, 8.36 inches wide, and weighs 2.8 pounds, which is 0.2 pounds lighter than the 13-inch MacBook Pro.

The M1 MacBook Air has a 13-inch display with a small black frame. Its design is similar to that of the MacBook Pro.

Display

As of 2018, the Retina display used by the MacBook Air has been redesigned, brighter, and clearer than the previous non-Retina display. The MacBook Air has a resolution of 2560 x 1600, 227 pixels per inch, has more than 4 million pixels, and a maximum brightness of 400 numbers.

The MacBook Air display supports True Tone, which is designed to adjust the color of the display to match the lighting in the room. True Tone works with a bright multi-channel light sensor installed on the MacBook Air model, which can determine the brightness and color temperature of the room.

After getting a white balance, the MacBook Air can adjust the color and intensity of the display to match the lighting in the room, leading to natural, paper-like tests, and can also reduce eye fatigue.

This year's new product is P3 Wide's color support, which can bring brighter and more vibrant colors, and is the development of sRGB color in the previous model. Wide color provides 25% more color than sRGB.

Keyboard

The IM1 MacBook Air uses a redesigned magic keyboard, first introduced on the 16-inch MacBook Pro and the previous-generation MacBook Air. The Magic Keyboard eliminates the way Apple has been using butter since 2015 because it is full of problems with significant failures due to dust and other small particles. , which can save a lot of energy, so that the button response is more sensitive.

The scissors on the MacBook Air keyboard can provide 1mm of

key movement and a stable key feel.

Apple has redesigned the M1 MacBook Pro keyboard to replace existing operating keys. Startup keypad and keyboard light controls have been replaced by highlighted search, call, and "Do not disturb", in addition to the emoji Fn key.

The keyboard also has illuminated buttons controlled by a wide light sensor, which can illuminate keys in a dark room.

Touch ID

The M1 MacBook Air Touch ID sensor is located next to the operating keys above the keyboard. Touch ID is powered by Secure Enclave, which ensures the security of your fingerprint data and personal information.

The Touch ID on the MacBook can be used instead of a password, and the Mac can be unlocked by placing your finger on the sensor. It can also enter passwords for password-protected apps and can be used to purchase Apple Pay Safari.

Trackpad

The MacBook Air is unarmed with a great Force Touch trackpad. The trackpad does not have traditional buttons but is powered by a set of Force Sensors, which allows users to press anywhere on the trackpad to get the same response.

The magnetic-powered Taptic engine gives users a touchable effect when using the touchpad, thus replacing the sensor of body buttons. The Force Touch trackpad supports light pressure (this is a regular click) and then presses deep or "force force" (as a separate action), which can provide definitions of highlighted words.

Ports

The MacBook Air contains two USB-C Thunderbolt 3 / USB-4 ports. With Thunderbolt 3, the MacBook Air can support 4K, 5K, and 6K displays, and connect to an eGPU was necessary to achieve faster graphics processing power.

The 6K display allows the M1 MacBook Air to be used with the Pro Display XDR and other 6K displays. MacBook Air supports one 6K display, one 5K display, or two 4K displays.

Apple said the M1 MacBook Pro is limited to single monitors with up to 6K resolution or two monitors with 4K resolution, but with the DisplayPort adapter, M1 MacBook Air and MacBook Pro models can launch up to five external displays. This can only happen when you mix 4K and 1080p displays because the Thunderbolt port does not have the bandwidth to start five 4K displays.

With more than two Thunderbolt 3 ports, there is also a 3.5 mm jack phone jack on one side of the device. Besides, there are no other ports on the MacBook Air, with Apple removing the USB-A port and SD card from MacBook Air models before 2018.

M1 Apple Silicon Chip

The MacBook Air is an Arm-based chip designed for Apple, one of the Macs' first updated, replacing the Intel chip similar to the previous MacBook Air model. These chips are called "Apple Silicon", and the chip used on the MacBook Air is the M1

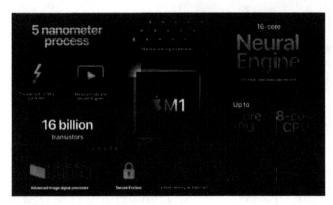

The M1 is the first chip system designed for Apple for Mac, which means it has a processor, GPU, O / O, security features, and RAM, and there is only one chip on the Mac. Apple said this could provide better performance and energy efficiency, thus increasing battery life.

Like Apple's latest A14 chip, the M1 is made using a 5-nanometer processor, making it smaller and more efficient than Apple's predecessors. With 16 billion transistors, Apple claims to be the largest transistor invested in a single chip.

Unified Memory Architecture

One of M1's functions is integrated memory, namely UMA, which combines high bandwidth, low latency memory. This means that the technology on the M1 chip can access the same data without copying it between multiple memory pools, which greatly improves the performance of the entire system.

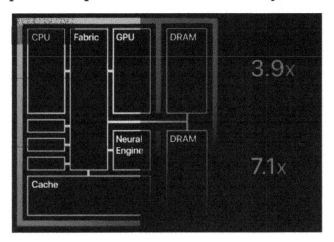

With UMA, the video editing speed increased 3.9 times, and the image processing speed increased by 7.1 times x faster.

Speed improvements

The M1 has an 8-core CPU and an 8-core GPU integrated (there is also a 7-core GPU option, as described below). The CPU has four very efficient characters and four cores of high performance. When performing simple tasks such as browsing the web or reading emails, the MacBook Air will use a high-performance core to extend battery life, but for system-enhancing functions such as photo and video editing, it will work for high performance.

Compared to high-performance cores, efficient cores use up to one-tenth of the power while still providing the performance required by Mac users for daily tasks.

According to Apple, the CPU speed of the M1 chip is 3.5 times that of the Intel chip on the previous MacBook Air, while the GPU speed is also five times higher. The basic MacBook Air model is fitted with an M1 chip with a 7-core GPU, while the high-end models with 512GB of high-end embedded 8-core GPU, similar to the M1 MacBook Pro and Mac mini.

Compared to competing for notebook chips, the M1 is designed to provide high performance at all levels of power. Compared to the latest PC notebook chips, its CPU performance has increased by 2 times, while power consumption has been reduced by 25%. In the GFX Bench 5.0 bench test, the M1 beat the GTX 1050 Ti and Radeon RX 560 with a 2.6 TFLOP output.

GPU	Manhattan	T-Rex	ALU 2	Driver Overhead 2	Texturing
Apple M1	407.7 FPS	660.1 FPS	298.1 FPS	245.2 FPS	71,149 MTexels/s
GeForce GTX 1050 Ti	288.3 FPS	508.1 FPS	512.6 FPS	218.2 FPS	59,293 MTexels/s
Radeon RX 560	221.0 FPS	482.9 FPS	6275.4 FPS	95.5 FPS	22,8901 MTexels/s

Gpu

The 8-core GPU on the M1 chip is integrated (which means it's not an independent chip), and Apple calls it the world's most integrated graphics on your computers. It can extract 25,000 threads at a time and combine advanced graphics performance with low power consumption.

Neural Engine

There is a new, more advanced engine on the MacBook Air that can increase the speed of machine learning tasks 9 times. The neural engine uses a 16-core design that can perform 11 trillion jobs per second and works with machine learning accelerators to perform ML-based tasks faster.

Neural engines can benefit programs such as Final Cut Pro, Pixelmator, etc. that use video learning, image, and audio editing.

No fan

The MacBook Air sort out not have a fan for cooling commitments. Instead, an aluminum radiator can dissipate heat to get a quiet operation. Compared to the older model, this is one of the only internal changes to the new MacBook Air.

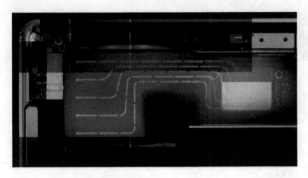

Running application

The M1 chip is based on the Arm architecture instead of the x96 build as an Intel chip, but thanks to Rosetta 2 (a back-end and invisible user interface), it can still run applications designed for Intel devices.

Apple also encourages developers to create universal applications that use a single binary file and run Apple's silicon Mac and Intel Mac. Besides, Apple Silicon Macs can launch apps designed for the iPhone and iPad.

We provide detailed information about updated apps with traditional or universal help, games on M1 Mac, customization programs, etc. See our M1 Highlights guide for details.

Battery life

With the improved performance of the M1, the battery life of the MacBook Air is impressive, significantly surpassing the battery life of the previous model.

Now, the same 49.9 WHr battery as the previous model can last up to 15 hours when browsing the web, and up to 18 hours when watching movies via the Apple TV app.

Performance testing

In the test when compiling WebKit open source code, Apple's M1 chip did well. The coding speed of the M1 MacBook Pro and Mac-

Book Air is faster than similar products based on Intel, but it is noteworthy that at the end of the test, the battery life is still 91%, and the battery life of the Intel 13-inch MacBook Pro is only 24%. on the left.

Connectivity

MacBook Air supports 802.11ax WiFi (called Wi-Fi 6), the latest WiFi protocol is faster and more efficient than the previous generation 802.11ac WiFi. It also supports Bluetooth 5.0.

Speaker and microphone

The MacBook Air uses stereo speakers with extensive stereo audio support to watch Apple TV+ content or play iOS games and has a three-way directional microphone for FaceTime calls.

FaceTime camera

A 720p HD camera is built into the front of the MacBook Air for FaceTime calls. Apple has used the 720p front camera for several years, but its quality has not improved, but this year it said the

M1 chip can provide clearer images.

The M1 chip provides better noise reduction to make shadows and highlights more detailed, while the neural engine uses facial recognition to adjust the white balance and exposure of natural skin tones.

storage

MacBook Air uses solid storage space with a maximum capacity of 2 TB. The basic storage capacity of the MacBook Air is 256GB, and the speed of the MacBook Air SSD is twice that of the previous generation SSD.

The SSD workbench ensures that the SSD of the MacBook Air is indeed very fast, with a writing speed of 2190MB/s and a reading speed of 2676MB/s. This is almost twice the SSD of the previous generation MacBook Air.

Get started

Set up your MacBook Air

When you start your MacBook Air for the first time, Setup Assistant will guide you through the simple steps needed to start using your new Mac.

Tip: Press the Escape key to learn to set up your Mac with Voice-

Over. Press Command-Option-F5 to view accessibility options. To learn more, see Available on Mac.

Select a country or region to set the language and period of your Mac. You can answer all commands, or skip certain commands, and select "Set Later" when you see an option. For example, after the initial setup, it may make sense to set up Apple Pay which requires a valid credit card and screen time that can be set by different users. Continue to learn more details about installation tasks.

- Connect to a Wi-Fi network: Select a network and enter the password as required. (If you are using Ethernet, you can also select other network options.) To change the network in the future, click the Wi-Fi status icon or control center in the menu bar, click "Other Networks", then select Wi-Fi network and enter a password. You can also choose to turn on or off Wi-Fi here.

Tip: After setup, if you can't see the Wi-Fi status icon in the menu bar, you can add it. Open System Preferences and click Network. Click Wi-Fi in the list on the left, then select "Show Wi-Fi Status in Menu Bar".

- Transfer details: If you want to set up a new computer and have not set up your Mac before, click "Do not transfer any information now". If you want to transfer data from another computer now or in the future, see Transfer data to the new MacBook Air.

- Sign in with your Apple ID: Your Apple ID has an email address and password. This is the account you use to manage Apple news, including using the App Store, Apple TV apps, Apple Book Store, Cloud, Messages, etc. Sign in with the same Apple ID to use any Apple app on any device, whether your computer, iOS device, iPadOS device, or Apple Watch. It's best to have your Apple ID and not share it. If you do not have an Apple ID, you can create it during the installation process (free). See Apple account on Mac.
- Screenshot: Monitor and receive computer use reports. For choices and details, see "Display Time" on Mac.
- Enable Siri and "Hey Siri": You can turn on Siri and "Hey Siri" during the setup process (to specify Siri requests). To enable "Hey Siri", say a few Siri commands when prompted. To learn how to unlock Siri and "Hey Siri" over time and for information about using Siri on Mac, check out Siri on Mac.
- Save files to iCloud: With iCloud, you can store all content (documents, movies, music, photos, etc.) in the cloud and access it anytime, anywhere. Be sure to sign in with the same Apple ID on all devices. To set this option later, open "System Preferences" and log in with your Apple ID. Click Apple ID, click Cloud in the sidebar, and select the function you want to use. To learn more, see Access iCloud content on Mac.
- Select Appearance: Select "Light", "Dark" or "Default" in desktop view. If you want to change the selection you made during the installation process, open System Preferences, click General, and select the Appearance option. You can also set some preferences here.
- Set Touch ID: You can add fingerprints to Touch ID during the setup process. To set up Touch ID or add more fingerprints later, open "System Preferences" and click on "Touch ID". To add a fingerprint, click the Insert but-

ton and follow the instructions on the screen.

You can also set up options on how to use Touch ID on Mac-Book Air: unlock Mac, use Apple Pay (see using Apple Pay on Mac), purchase items in the App Store, Apple TV App, Apple Book Store, on the website, and fill in your password automatically.

Tip: If two or more users use the same MacBook Air, each user can add fingerprints to the Touch ID to quickly open, authenticate and log into the MacBook Air. Each user account can add up to three fingerprints, and all MacBook Air user accounts can add up to five fingerprints.

- Set up Apple Pay: During the setup process, you can set up an Apple Pay user account on your MacBook Air. Some users may still use Apple Pay to make payments, but they should use the iPhone nor Apple Watch set by Apple Pay to complete the purchase (see using Apple Pay on Mac). Follow the on-screen instructions to add and verify your card. If you have already used the card to purchase media, you may be told to verify the card first.

To set up Apple Pay or insert other cards later, open "System Preferences" and click on "Wallet with Apple Pay". Follow the on-screen instructions to set up Apple Pay.

Note: Card issuer decides whether your card meets Apple Pay usage terms and may require you to provide additional information to complete the verification process. Numerous credit and debit cards can be used with Apple Pay. For details on the availability of Apple Pay and current credit card providers, please refer to the Apple Ap sponsorship article Please pay with participating banks.

Tip: If you are unfamiliar with Mac, please see the Apple Support Mac Mac Tips article for Windows Switcher and What's the name on Mac? You can check out Mac Macs' quick tour for more details.

Apple account on Mac

Your Apple ID is an account that allows you to access all Apple services. Use your Apple ID to download apps from the App Store; access media in Apple Music, Apple Podcast, Apple TV, and Apple Books; use iCloud to keep content up to date on all devices; set up a family sharing group; and more.

You can similarly use your Apple ID to access other apps and websites (see "Log in with Apple on Mac" in the macOS User Guide).

Important Note: If you forget your Apple ID password, you do not need to create a new Apple ID. Just click the "Forgot Apple ID or password?" In the login window to recover your secret code.

If other family members use Apple devices, make sure each family member has their own Apple ID. You can create your child's Apple ID account and share purchases and subscriptions with "Family Sharing", which will be explained later in this section.

To view available Apple ID services, see Where can I use Apple ID?

All in one place. Manage everything related to your Apple ID in one place. Open System Preferences on your MacBook Air with your Apple ID and Family Sharing settings are on top.

Update account, security, and payment details. In "System Preferences", click on "Apple ID" and select an item in the sidebar to view and update the details associated with your account.

- Overview: The "View All" window lets you know that your account is set up and running; if not, you will see tips and notifications here.
- Name, Phone, Email: Update the name and contact details associated with your Apple ID. You can also manage Apple email subscriptions.
- Password and security: Change your Apple ID password, turn on two-factor authentication, add or remove trusted phone numbers, and create sign-in verification

codes on another device or iCloud.com. You can also bring about which apps and websites use "Log in with Apple". See "Log in with Apple" in the macOS user monitor.

- Payment and Delivery: Manage payment methods associated with Apple ID and shipping address from the Apple Store.
- ICloud: Check the box next to the iCloud function to enable the function. When iCloud is enabled, your content is stored on iCloud instead of locally on your Mac, so you can access any content on any device with iCloud unlocked with the same Apple ID.
- Media and Purchases: Manage accounts associated with Apple Music, Apple Podcast, Apple TV, and Apple Books; select purchase settings; and manage your subscription.

View all your devices. Under the Apple ID sidebar, view all devices connected to Apple ID. You can check if "Find My Device" is open on each device (see "Find My Device"), check the Cloud Backup status for iOS or iPadOS devices, or if you are no longer the owner of the device, start to Remove Device from on account.

Family sharing. By sharing families, you can set up family groups and create Apple ID accounts for your children. To manage your family sharing settings, click "Family Sharing" in "System Preferences" and select the icon in the sidebar to view and update your details. You can add or remove family members; share media purchases, payment methods, iCloud storage, and your location; and set the child time limit (see Screen time on Mac).

Learn more. To learn more about iCloud and family sharing, see Access iCloud content on Mac and Manage family sharing groups on Mac in the macOS User Guide.

Find your way around

Desktop, menu bar, and help on Mac

The first thing you see on a MacBook Air is a desktop, where you can quickly open programs, search anything on the MacBook Air and the Web, edit files, etc.

Tip: Can't find the screen on the screen? To zoom in a moment, quickly move your finger back and forth on the trackpad. Or, if you use a mouse, slide the mouse back and forth quickly.

Menu bar. The menu bar works at the top of the screen. Use the left-hand menu to select commands and perform tasks in the application. Menu items will change depending on the application you are using. Use the icon on the right to connect to a Wi-Fi network, check your Wi-Fi status icon, open the "Control Center", and click the "Control Center" icon, check that the battery is fully charged. , then use Spotlight to search for the Spotlight icon, etc.

Tip: You can change the icon displayed in the menu bar. See control center on Mac.

Apple Menu. Apple's menu contains frequently used items and is always displayed in the upper left corner of the screen. To open it, click the Apple icon.

Application menu. You can open multiple applications and windows at once. The name of the active application will be displayed in bold on the right side of the Apple menu, and then the only menu for that application. When you open another application or click an open window in another application, the name of the app menu will change to that application, and the menu item will also change accordingly. If you are looking for a command in the menu and can't find the command, check the system menu to see if the system you want is working.

Help menu. MacBook Air support is always available in the menu bar. For help, open the Portal Finder, click the "Help" menu, then select "MacOS Help" to open the macOS User Guide. Or type in the search field and select suggestions. For specific app help, open the app and click "Help" in the menu bar.

For more information, please refer to the macOS User Guide.

Use stacks to stay organized. You can use desktops on a desktop to organize files into groups (by category, date, or tag) and keep the desktop clean. To view stack content, click the stack to expand its contents, or place the cursor on the stack to view file icons. To create a stack on the desktop, click on desktop and select View> Use Stack or press Control-Command-0. You can also hold the Control key and click on the desktop, then select "Use Stack". To view stack collection options, go to View> Group By, and select an option. After that, all new files you add to the desktop are automatically sorted into the appropriate stack. To learn more, see Organizing files in the file stack on Mac in the macOS User Guide.

Continue reading to learn about Finder on Mac and other desktop features.

Finder on Mac

Use Finder to organize and retrieve files. To open the Finder window, click the Finder icon in the Dock at the bottom of the screen. Force a file icon to quickly view its contents, or force a file name to edit.

Sync devices. When you connect a device such as an iPhone or iPad, you can see it in the Finder sidebar. From there you can backup, update, and restore the device

Gallery views. Using "Gallery View", you can see great previews of selected files, giving you a quick way to visually view photos, video clips, and other documents. The preview window displays details that help you identify the file you need. Use the wash bar at the bottom to quickly find what you need. To close or open the preview window, press Shift-Command-P.

Tip: To display the file name in "Gallery View", press Command-J and select "Show Name File".

Take immediate action. In the lower right corner of the "Preview" shortcut window lets you manage and edit files directly in the Finder. You can rotate images in "Marks", interpret or crop

photos, combine photos and PDFs into a single file, cut audio and video files, and create custom actions (for example, watermark files) with Automator's workflow.

To show Preview options in Finder, select View> Show Preview. To customize the displayed content, select View> Preview Options, and then select your file type options. See Perform quick actions on Finder on Mac in macOS User Guide.

Tip: Select a file and press the space bar to open "Quick Get". You can sign the PDF; cut audio and video files; then tag, rotate, and crop photos without opening a separate app. To learn more about the "Quick Find" and "Mark" functions, see Use Quick Find to view and edit files on Mac and "Mark files on Mac" in the macOS User Guide.

Dock on Mac

Dock at the bottom of the screen is an easy place to store programs and documents that you use regularly.

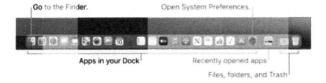

Open the program or file. Click the app icon in Dock, or click the launchpad icon in Dock to view all the apps on your Mac, and then click the app you want. You can also use Spotlight (in the upper right corner of the menu bar) to search for an app, and then open the app directly from Spotlight search results. Recently opened applications will be displayed in the middle section of the Dock.

Close the app. When you click the red dot in the upper left corner of the open window, the window closes, but the app stays open. In Dock, there is a black dot under the open app. To close an application, select "Exit in Application Name" from the application menu (for example, in the "Email" application, select "Exit Email" from the "Email" menu). Or press the Control key and click the Application icon in Dock, then click "Exit".

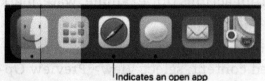

Indicates an open app

Insert the object into Dock. Drag and drop the item to the wanted location. Install the application on the left side of the Dock, then insert the file or folder on the right.

Remove item from Dock. Drag and drop out Dock. This item will not be removed from the MacBook Air, but will only be removed from the Port.

View all open content on your Mac. Press the control key on the keyboard, or swipe with three fingers on the touchpad to turn on the machine control. View open windows, desktop space, full-screen apps, etc., and easily switch between them. You can also add task control icons to Dock. Please see the Apple Support article Using "Task Control" on Mac.

View all windows open in the app. Force click on the Dock app to access Exposé and view all open windows for that app.

Tip: Click Dock and the menu preferences menu to change Dock's appearance and behavior. Zoom in or out of the Document, move it to the left or right of the screen, set it to hide when not in use, etc.

Learn more. See Using Dock on Mac in the macOS User Directory.

Notification Center on Mac

The notification center has been redesigned to place all important details, reminders, and widgets in one convenient location. Find detailed information on calendar events, stocks, weather, etc., and receive notifications (emails, messages, reminders, etc.) that you may miss.

Click to open
Notification Center.

Open the notification center. Click the date or time in the top right corner of the screen, or use two fingers to swipe left from the right edge of the trackpad. Scroll down to see more.

Share your notifications. Reply to emails, listen to recent podcasts, or view detailed information on calendar events. Click the arrow in the top right corner of the notification to view options, take action, or get more information.

Customize your widget. Click Edit Widgets to add, delete or rearrange widgets. You can also add third-party doodad from the Mac App Store.

Set your notification preferences. Open Method Preferences and click Notices to select which notices you see. Notifications are updated recently, and the redesigned "Today" widget brings details at a glance.

Learn more. See Apple support article Using notifications on Mac.

Control Center on Mac

The new "Control Center" integrates all the other functions of your menu bar in one place, allowing you to quickly access most commonly used controls, such as Bluetooth, AirDrop, screen, and light and volume controls, directly from the menu bar. Click the

Control Center icon in the top right corner of the screen to open the control center.

Click for more options. Click the button to see more options. For example, click the Wi-Fi button to view your favorite network, other networks or open "Network Favorites" To return to the main control center view, click the Control Center icon again.

Pin your "Control Center" preferences. Drag your favorite item from the "Control Center" to the menu bar anywhere, so you can easily access it with a single click. To adjust the content displayed in the control center and menu bar, open the Quay & Menu Bar Preferences, select the controller on the left, and then click "Show in Menu Bar" or "Show in Control Center". You will see the controls will appear at a preview in the menu bar. Some items cannot be added or removed from the control center or menu bar.

Tip: To quickly remove an item from the menu bar, grab the Command key and drag it out of the menu.

Click a feature to view where it appears.

Select "Show in Menu Bar" to see a feature's location in the menu bar.

The feature's location is highlighted in Control Center.

Learn more. See Use Mac Control Center in MacOS User Guide. See also.

AirDrop on Mac and AirPlay on Mac

System preferences on Mac

System preferences are when you customize your MacBook Air settings. For instance, use battery preferences to adjust sleep settings. Or use the "Desktop and Screen Server" preferences to add a desktop image or select screen saver.

Customize your MacBook Air. Click the "System Favorites" icon in the Dock, or select the "Apple" menu> "System Favorites". Then click the type of predilection you want to set. To study more, see "Modify Mac With System First choice" in the macOS User Guide.

Specify what Spotlight searches on your Mac.

Set preferences for VoiceOver, Zoom, and other options.

Arrange multiple displays, set resolution and brightness, and more.

Update macOS. In System Preferences, click Software Update to see if your Mac is using the latest version of macOS software. You can specify automatic software update options.

Focus on Mac

Spotlight The Spotlight icon is an easy way to find anything on your MacBook Air, such as documents, contacts, calendar events, and emails. Exposure suggestions provide information from Wikipedia articles, web search results, news, sports, weather, stocks, movies, and other sources.

Search for anything. Click the Spotlight icon at the top right of the screen and start typing.

Tip: Type Command-Spacebar to show or hide the Spotlight search field.

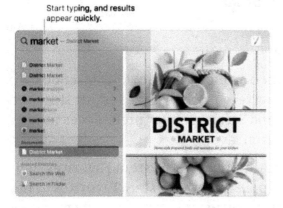

Change currencies and metrics. Enter the amount (for example, $, € or ¥) with the amount, and press the Return key to get a list of converted prices. Or specify a unit of measurement conversion measurement.

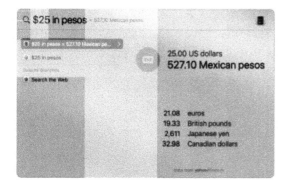

Open the app. Enter a request name in Spotlight and press Return.

Turn off Spotlight suggestions. If you want Attention to search only on MacBook Air, open "System Fondness", click "Spotlight", and then click "Siri Suggestions." You can also make some changes to the list of visual search categories.

Learn more. See you using Spotlight on Mac in macOS User Guide.

Siri on Mac

You can talk to Siri on your MacBook Air and use your voice to perform many tasks. For example, you can find files, schedule meetings, change preferences, get feedback, send messages, make calls, and add items to your calendar. Siri can give you directives ("How do I get home from here?"), Give you details ("How high is Mount Whitney?"), Perform basic tasks ("craft a fresh menu"), and more.

If the "Listen to 'Hey Siri'" option is enabled for Siri preferences, Siri will be presented as long as you say "Hey Siri" and immediately state your request.

Note: To use Siri, your Mac must be connected to the Internet. Siri may not be presented in all languages or regions, and types may vary by region.

Enable S hour. Open System Preferences, click Siri and set options. If Siri is enabled during the setup process, press and hold the call / Fire key (F5) key microphone to turn on Siri. Or click Siri on the system preferences, and select Allow to ask Siri. You can set some preferences in the Siri window, such as the language and voice you must use, and that you can show Siri in the menu bar.

Talk to Siri. Press and hold the call / Siri key (F5) and the microphone key, or press and hold the Command-Spacebar (or say "Hey Siri" when the feature is turned on), and start talking. You can add a Siri icon to the menu bar by selecting this option in the Siri window for system preferences. Then click the Siri icon to apply Siri.

Hello Siri. On MacBook Air, you can simply say "Hello Siri" to get an answer to your request. To enable this feature in the Siri System Preferences window, click "Listen to Hi Siri" and say a few Siri commands when prompted.

For convenience, "Hey Siri" does not respond when the MacBook Air lid is closed. When the door is closed and connected to an external display, you can still call Siri in the left menu icon.

Tip: To learn more about how to use Siri, please ask "What can you do?" You can click the "Help" button at any time.

play music. Just say "play music" and Siri does something else. You can tell Siri: Play well know songs from March 1991."

Find and open the file. Let Siri find the files and open them directly from the Siri window. You can ask by file name or description.

Drag and drop. Drag and drop a photo and a location from the Siri window into an email, text message, or document. You can copy and paste the text.

Change the voice. Click Siri on the system preferences, then selects an option from the Siri voice menu.

In this guide, you'll find Siri suggestions, which look like this:

Ask Siri. Say this:

- Exposed the conversation of the day I was performing past night"
- What time is it in Paris?"

Learn more. See Apple's backing article "How to Use Siri on Mac".

Mac Display Settings

Align the surrounding light. Your MacBook Air has a Retina display with TrueTone® technology. True Tone will automatically adjust the color of the display to match your natural light to provide a natural viewing experience. In the "Show" window of "System Preferences", turn on or off "Real Tone".

Use a powerful desktop. If you use a powerful desktop image, the desktop image will automatically change to match the time of day in your area. Click "Desktop and Screen Saver" in "System Fondness", click on "Desktop", and select the "Active Desktop" image. To change the screen depending on the time zone, please enable location services. When "Location Tasks" is turned off, the image will change according to the time zone specified in the "Date and Time" preferences.

Use the black mode to stay focused. You can use the black desktop scheme, menu bar, Dock, and all built-in MacOS apps. Your content is highlighted in the front and center, while dimmed controls and windows reverse. You see white text in dark background in apps such as "Email", "Contacts", "Calendar" and "Messages", so your vision will be easier when working in a dark place.

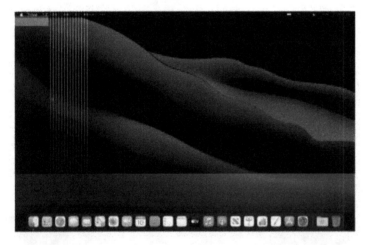

The dark mode is for professionals who edit photos and images - colors and fine details will appear in the background of the black app. Also great for those who just want to focus on their content.

Connect the monitor. See Use an external monitor on MacBook

Air.

Learn more. See Apple's support article "Using Retina Display".

Transfer data to the new MacBook Air

It's easy to move files and settings from any Mac or PC to MacBook Air. You can transfer data to your MacBook Air from your old computer (or from a Time Machine backup to a USB storage device) wirelessly or using a cable and Ethernet adapter.

You may need to upgrade the MacOS version to your old computer before transferring data. Migration Assistant needs MacOS 10.7 or higher, but it's best to update old computers to the latest version. If you're not sure if you own a MacBook Air or want to find out more about other models, see the Apple support article "Find the MacBook Air Model."

Tip: For best results, make sure your new MacBook Air uses the latest version of macOS. Open System Preferences and click Software Update to check for updates.

Move from PC to Mac. If you are unfamiliar with Mac and want to transfer from a Windows computer, please refer to the transfer of information from PC to Mac in the macOS user guide and Apple support article Transferring your data from Windows PC to Mac.

Wireless transmission. To transfer data when you set up your MacBook Air for the first time, use Setup Assistant. To move information later, please use the Migration Assistant. Open the Finder window, go to "Applications", open "Applications", and double-click "Migration Assistant" to make wireless migration. Follow the instructions on the screen.

Tip: To wirelessly transfer data from an old computer to a Mac-Book Air, make sure both computers are connected to the same network. During the entire migration process, the two computers were close together.

If you use Time Machine to back up files from another Mach to storage (such as an external disk), you can copy files from that device to a MacBook Air. See Back up and Restore the Mac.

Copy files from USB storage. Use USB-C on a USB adapter to connect a storage device to a MacBook Air (see MacBook Air accessories). Then drag the file from the storage device to the MacBook Air.

Use Ethernet transmission. To transfer data via Ethernet, use an adapter (available separately) to connect an Ethernet cable to a MacBook Air. Connect the other end of the Ethernet cable to another computer (if your computer does not have an Ethernet port, you may need another adapter). Before using Ethernet to transfer data, make sure the MacBook Air battery is fully charged.

Restore your content. To learn how to restore a Mac from Time Machine or other backups, see the Apple Support Recovery Mac backup article.

Learn more. See the macOS User Guide to transfer data from another computer or device to a Mac, as well as the Apple support article on How to Transfer Content to a New Mac.

Back up and restore the Mac

To ensure file security, it is important to back up your MacBook Air regularly. An easy way to backup is to backup your apps, accounts, preferences, music, photos, movies, and texts using Time Machine built in to your Mac (doesn't back up the macOS app). Use Time Machine to back up an external storage device connected to a MacBook Air or supported network volume. For a list of devices supported by Time Machine, see the Apple support article Backup Disks that can be used with Time Machine.

Tip: You can use the Mac shared on the same network as the MacBook Air as your storage location. On another Mac, go to the "Share" "Favorites" window and open "File Sharing". To add a shared folder, hold Control and click the folder, select "Advanced Options", then click "Share as Time Machine Backup Destination".

Set the timer. Make sure the MacBook Air and external storage device are on the same Wi-Fi network or connect an external storage device to the MacBook Air. Open "System Preferences", click on "Machine Time", and select "Auto Backup". Select the drive you want to use for backup, and everything is ready.

Use iCloud backup. Files in iCloud Drive and photos in iCloud Photos are automatically saved to iCloud and do not need to be part of a Time Machine backup. However, if you want to back up, do the following:

- iCloud Drive: Open System Preferences, click Apple ID,

then click on iCloud and select "Configure Mac Storage". Cloud Drive content will be stored on Mac and backed up.

- iCloud Photos: Open Photos and select Photos> Preferences. In the "iCloud" window, select "Real Download on this Mac." The full version of the image library optimization will be stored on Mac and backed up.

Restore files. You can use Time Machine to retrieve all files at once. Click the Time Machine icon in the menu bar and select Enter Time Machine. (If there is no "Time Machine" icon in the menu bar, select "Apple Menu"> "System Favorites", click "Time Machine", and then select "Show Time Machine in the menu bar".) Select one or more items to be restored (one folder or all disk), and then click Restore.

If you use Time Machine to back up your Mac, you can restore files if an application or boot disk is damaged. To do this, you must install macOS on your Mac before using a Time Machine backup to restore files. Read on for more details.

Reinstall macOS. Active system files and personal files are stored on a separate system disk. However, some tasks (such as wiping or accidentally damaging a disk) require you to restore your MacBook Air. You can reinstall macOS and use Time Machine to restore your files from backup. There are several ways to restore a Mac with macOS Big Sur. It may be necessary to install a higher version of macOS than the original version with your computer or a version used before disk damage. To learn more about these options, refer to the macOS user guide to get all the files from the Time Machine backup and the Apple support Article How to restore MacOS to MacOS restore.

Important: Advanced users may want to create a bootable installer to install macOS in the future. This is useful if you want to use some form of macOS. See the Apple support article How to create a stumbling block for macOS.

Learn more. See the macOS User Guide to Use Time Machine on

Mac to back up files with Time Machine troubleshooting, and the Apple support article What to do before selling, donating, or trading a Mac.

Availability on Mac

Your Mac, iOS, and iPadOS device include powerful tools that make Apple product features accessible and easy for everyone to use. Mac has four access points to focus on. Click the link to learn more about the features of each location:

- Just think
- Hearing
- Liquid
- Read

For more information on Apple's accessibility support, please visit Availability.

Accessibility preferences. In the "System Preferences" preferences, "Accessibility" is now set to visual, audio and sports themes, making it easy to find what you need.

Use voice control to complete all tasks. You can only control your Mac with audio. All voice processing voice control is done on the device, so your data will be kept private.

Accurate call. If you cannot enter text by hand, accurate pronunciation is essential for communication. Voice control brings the latest advances in machine learning in speech-to-text writing.

You can add custom words to help control the voice to see your frequently used words. Select "System Preferences"> "Accessibility", select "Voice Control", then click on "Vocabulary" and enter the words you want. To customize the commands on the Voice Control Preferences page, click Commands and choose to save the default commands or add new commands.

Note: Improved pronunciation accuracy only applies to American English.

Editing rich text. RTF editing commands in voice control allow you to make quick adjustments and then proceed to express your next thought. You can change one phrase to another, quickly set the cursor to edit, and select the text correctly. Attempt "joy is just outside" instead of "Joy is coming". When correcting words, word suggestions and emojis can help you quickly choose what you need.

Perfect navigation. Use voice commands to open and interact with applications. To click on an item, simply specify its accessibility label name. You can also say "show numbers" to see the number labels next to all the clicks, then say the number you want to click. If you need to touch a part of the screen without controls, you can say "show grid" to hover the grid on the screen and perform tasks such as clicking, zoom in, drag, etc.

Move up and zoom in. Use the navigation text to display the text's high definition text below the cursor. When you hover your mouse over the text, press the Command key, and a window with enlarged text appears on the screen.

The beautiful hibiscus plant is a fine ingredient in teas and desserts. It's also supposedly good for high cholesterol, something NOLA folks have too

The zoom indicator allows you to zoom in on one monitor, while the other maintains its standard resolution. View the same screen at a nearby distance and at the same time.

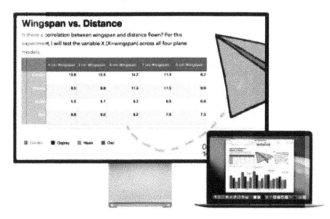

Use VoiceOver Siri. If you like Siri's natural sound, you can choose to use VoiceOver Siri or voice Siri. Simplified keyboard navigation requires less drilling in a separate focus group, making it easier to navigate with VoiceOver. You can also save custom typing icons on the Cloud and select from the international braille table. Also, if you are an engineer, VoiceOver can now read line numbers, breakpoints, alerts, and errors in the Xcode text editor.

Color enhancement. If you do not see the color correctly, you can use the new color filter option to adjust the display color of your

Mac. You can easily turn on or off this preference using the "Accessibility" panel to quickly distinguish colors, and you can access this panel by pressing Touch ID three times.

Learn more. See Using Mac Accessibility Features in the macOS User Guide.

New features of MacBook Air

The MacBook Air has powerful performance, can run your favorite programs faster than ever, and advanced technology including Wi-Fi 6 and Thunderbolt / USB 4. Keyboard upgrades include shortcuts that can be used for Spotlight and call functions. See the MacBook Air Magic Keyboard with Touch ID.

macOS Big Sur introduces a new look for the Mac desktop, designed to integrate Apple devices. The new design includes a flexible base and menu, updated but custom icons, and a wide menu. The full height sidebar and the integrated toolbar buttons make the app easy to use. Even the sound you hear when you receive a notification or alarm has been updated.

The new design makes navigation easier and gives you more control over the following features:

- Control Center: The new Control Center puts all your favorite menu items in one place, so you can quickly access the most widely used controls and preferences (such as Wi-Fi, AirDrop, and Bluetooth). See control center on Mac.
- Notification Center: A redesigned notification center shows your notifications and widgets in one column. You can customize the widgets you see and share notifications (for example, reply to emails)

The "weather" widget is accurate and warns of bad weather or major changes. Please check the notification center on your Mac.

In addition to the redesigned look, macOS Big Sur also includes significant improvements to these apps:

- Safari: Sin Attempt "joy is just outdoor" as an alternative to "Joy is upcoming" Safari was first released in 2003, it is the largest update to Safari, providing an instant browsing experience. Make your browsing experience richer with the new customizable homepage, and get many more extensions in the App Store. Use the brand new Favicon on the label and the label preview from there to scroll up for easy browsing. Click on the translation icon to quickly translate web pages into 7 supported languages (beta). Safari also provides a new privacy report showing how you are protecting your privacy on various websites you are browsing. Safari has become the world's fastest desktop browser. Provides faster browsing and uploading of frequently visited websites than Chrome or Firefox. See Safari.

- Map: The newly selected guide can help you find the best places to eat, shop, and visit, and you can make your guide. Use "See Around" 3D matching tours of selected city streets. You can now set up a bike path that gives you directions to altitudes and obstacles, or an electric bike route, with charging stops and timing. The indoor map is ideal for large airports and shopping areas, so you can easily find restaurants, toilets, and shops. See the map.

- Messaging: New tools make it easy to share and display messages and manage group chats. With the new message effect, you can customize the message with balloons, confetti, etc. Add Memoji stickers that match your mood and personality to the conversation, and use the Memoji editor on your Mac to create new stickers. You can even instantly share GIFs or best photos in your photo library with # images and a new photo clip. The new group messaging feature makes communication easier with family, friends, and colleagues. Pin your favorite conversations at the top of the address list for quick access. Use in-line responses to directly respond to messages, and send messages directly to individuals in group conversations by simply typing their names. Set photos or emojis in group discussions and share them with all group members. See message.

macOS Big Sur also offers the following new features and enhancements to existing features:

- AirPods: AirPods can switch seamlessly between active devices connected to the same iCloud account, making it easier to use AirPods and Apple devices. On a Mac, you can click the notification to change the audio from another device. Device switches can be used with AirPods Pro, AirPods (second generation), Powerbeats, Powerbeats Pro, and Beats Solo Pro. Requires an iPhone or iPod with the latest version of iOS; iPad with the latest version of iPadOS; or Mac with the latest version of macOS.

- Apple Arcade: See what games your Game Center friends are playing directly from the Arcade tab, and check out your achievements and objectives on the game page. Game Center now features an in-game dashboard, so you can see your progress with your friends at a glance. See App App.
- Battery: Your MacBook Air has now improved battery charging and battery power graphs and usage history. See Charging a MacBook Air battery.
- Family Sharing: An improved user interface for family settings makes family members clearer and can manage their family settings. Setting up a family, adding new members, and managing family details is easier than ever. See more details on family sharing in A.Access iCloud content to Mac and Apple accounts on Mac.
- Homepage: The "Homepage" app has some improvements, including visually impaired locations and a snapshot of attachments that require your attention or sharing important status changes, face recognition and functionality of door and camera doors, and flexible lighting. See homepage.
- iPhone and iPad apps on MacBook Air: Many iPhone and iPad apps can now run on MacBook Air. See App App.
- Listen Now: In "Music and Podcasts", the "Listen Now" tab lets you understand your preferences (favorite artists, chats, remixes, podcasts) and offer suggestions based on your listening content. The podcast features a more focused Up Next, so you can easily proceed to the next episode online. See music and podcasts.
- Notes: The new text style provides you with many note formatting options. Improved scanning functionality

on iPhone helps you to capture clear scans and transfer them to your Mac for immediate use. See note.

- Photos: Video and photo editing enhanced with filters, special effects, etc. You can refine your refined image and add captions to photos and videos. Memory enhancement features include many film and video enhancement music tracks. See pictures.

- Reminders: Separate tasks and get smart suggestions for using reminders in new ways. Give reminders to people who have shared the list with you and they will be notified. You can also let smart suggestions help you create reminders based on the same reminders created in the past. When you contact someone via Email, Siri will point out potential reminders and give you suggestions for creating them. Then use the new keyboard shortcut to quickly find the reminder you need. See reminder.

- Software Update: With macOS Big Sur, the software update starts in the background and the update speed is much faster than before, so it's easy to update your Mac and keep it safe.

- Brightness: Brightness is much faster than before. Now, it will highlight your top search results and suggestions as you type, so you can quickly access high-quality suggestions. Visual technology is also used in the "Discover" apps menu such as Safari, Pages, and Keynote. View brightness on Mac.

- Voice memo: Install folders to help you keep your voice memo organized. Easily mark the recordings as "favorites" so you can access them quickly later. With a single click, background sound can be reduced automatically, thus taking Voice Memos one step further. See voice memo.

Use MacBook Air with other devices

iCloud and continuity

When you create an Apple ID, you will automatically receive 5 GB of iCloud storage for free. You can use it for small things like backing up iPhone backups and syncing app data. You can use it for great things, like storing all your music and photos in the cloud and improving your Mac's storage. If 5 GB of storage is not enough, you only need to pay $ 0.99 a month to upgrade. When connecting Mac and iOS devices to iCloud, you can take advantage of Apple's Continuity feature, which allows you to start some content on one device and continue using it on another device.

> ➢ Learn exactly how to fix up and use iCloud on your Mac
> ➢ Learn about iCloud and your photos
> ➢ Learn about iCloud and your music
> ➢ Learn all about progress on Mac and iOS

How to set up iCloud on a Mac

If you're upgrading your Mac app or using your Mac for the first time, you'll be asked if you want to use iCloud Drive to store data. When you click "Yes", everything is ready. If you clicked "No" during the installation process, but now that you've decided to use Cloud Drive, you can still enable it manually.

1. Get on the Apple icon in the lower-left corner of the screen.
2. Select System Fondness ... from the drop-down menu.

3. Select Login in the top right corner.

4. Enter your Apple ID and password.

5. Click Next.

6. Select Allow to allow Find My Mac in the popup window.
7. Verify checkboxes next to all apps that use iCloud.

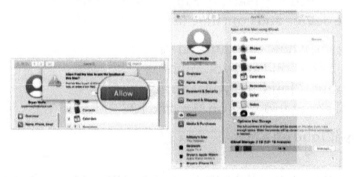

It is best to keep checkboxes for each application. This way, your settings will be applied to all your iCloud-enabled devices.

How to view your iCloud account details

You can check contact details, passwords and security, registered devices, and iCloud payment settings for iPhone, iPad, and Mac.

How to view your iCloud account details on Mac

1. Click the Apple icon in the lower-left corner of the screen.
2. Click System Fondness ... from the pull-down menu.
3. Click Apple ID at the top.

4. Click name, phone, email.

You can change the email address and phone number people can contact you with, and change the birthday. You can also enable email subscriptions for announcements about Apple products and popular news reports.

How to view password and security details on Mac

1. Click the Apple icon in the lower-left corner of the screen.
2. Click System Fondness ... from the pull-down menu
3. Click Apple ID at the top.

4. Click password and security.

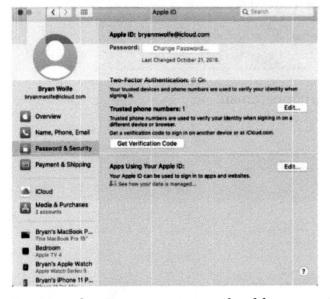

You can change your password, add a new phone number to a trusted number, and receive a verification code sent to you to sign in to other devices or iCloud.com.

How to view payment and shipping details on Mac

1. Click the Apple icon in the lower-left corner of the screen.
2. Click System First choice ... from the pull-down menu.
3. Click Apple ID at the top.

How to use the store on iCloud

"Storage in iCloud" allows you to store old photos, files, and messages in the cloud, freeing up space on your hard drive. The message will remain on the hard drive until the hard drive starts. If you run out of space, photos, files, and messages will be automatically saved to iCloud, and only the latest attachments will remain on your Mac for quick and easy access.

1. Click the Apple icon in the lower-left corner of the screen.
2. Select Almost This Mac from the drop-down menu.

3. Click the Storage tab in the system details window.
4. Click Manage.

5. Click "Store in iCloud" in the "Store" section in the "iCloud" window.
6. Click Store on iCloud again to confirm that you want to enable the feature to automatically store photos, files,

and messages in iCloud when the hard drive is full.

How to set up sync desktop folders with text in iCloud on Mac

If you've ever tried to sync "Desktop" and "Docs" folders to iCloud, but decided you don't like it, you can stop syncing. If sync is disabled, the desktop file will no longer appear on the Mac desktop computer, but it will still be in the file on Cloud Drive, and you can delete it. Your Documents folder is still visible in Cloud Drive, and you can move it.

1. Click the Apple icon in the top left corner of the Mac screen.
2. Select system preferences
3. Select Apple ID

4. Click "Options" next to "Cloud Drive."
5. Uncheck the "Desktop and Documents Folders" box.

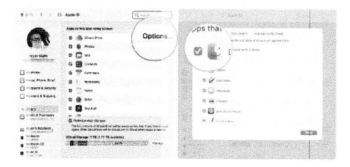

How to use Optimize Storage on Mac

Upgrading storage involves storing media in the cloud that is not already in iCloud storage, especially movies and TV programs that you have already watched on iTunes. When you choose to expand storage, we will delete these files from your computer. If you want to watch them again, you can download them again from iTunes.

It also gives you the option to store email attachments. You can set it to save the latest email attachments to your Mac, or you can save all email attachments to the cloud and download the required files when needed.

1. Click the Apple icon at the lower-left angle of the screen.
2. Select About This Mac from the menu.

3. Click the Storage tab in the system details window.
4. Click Manage.

5. Click "Optimize ..." in the "Arrange Storage" unit in the window.
6. Click Reset to confirm that you want to enable this feature to automatically delete iTunes movies and TV programs that you have watched.

How to disable enhanced storage on Mac

"Optimize Storage" will automatically delete iTunes movies and TV programs you have watched on your Mac. When the hard drive is finished, it will also save the latest email attachments to the Mac. If you want to save movies and TV shows to your hard drive so you don't have to download them every time you watch them, you can disable this feature.

1. Click the Apple icon in the top left corner of the Mac screen.
2. Select system preferences
3. Select Apple ID.

4. Click to uncheck the checkbox at the bottom of the "Prepare Mac Storage" window.

How to use empty trash automatically

It is common for regular computer users to forget to remove garbage regularly. Like a real garbage can, garbage cans will start to pile up. Unfortunately, unlike trash, Mac trash is not full, so you never know if you've been storing digital trash for months. Automatic dumping of the trash will enable a tool that will clear the contents of the trash for more than 30 days. You don't even need to think about it anymore.

1. Click the Apple icon in the lower-left corner of the screen.
2. Select Almost This Mac from the pop-up menu.

3. Click the Storage tab in the system details window.
4. Click Manage.

5. In the "Default Blank" section in the "Modified Storage" window, click "Open."
6. Click "Open" again to confirm that you want to qualify this feature to automatically erase files that ought to be in the trash for more than 30 days.

How to automatically disable garbage on Mac

If you are worried about deleting something on your Mac and need it back in 30 days, you can disable the feature and go back to sleep trash by hand.

1. Open a recovery window.
2. Click Finder in the top left corner of the Mac screen.
3. Select Favorites from the drop-down menu.
4. Select "Advanced" in the "Discover Preferences" window.

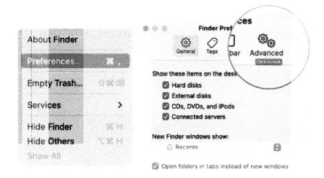

5. Click to uncheck the trash can in the back of the 30-day checkbox.

How to use it to reduce clutter

Reduce confusion is a feature in "Optimize Storage" that requires you to manually clean files on your Mac.

The section list on the left side of the "Optimize Storage" window shows folders that like to store old files and can be deleted on a Mac.

You can click "View Files" in the "Reduction Clutter" section of the "Configure storage" window, or you can select a category from the list on the left side of the window.

You can then browse the files one by one and decide if you want to save the files or delete them from your Mac.

For example, in the "Applications" folder, you can view applications on your Mac by type. The old version of the app you are currently using takes up 20 GB of space. You can delete files directly from the Customized Storage window. If you have Cloud Photo Library, how can you use photo storage?

How to use photo storage if you have Cloud Photo Library

Photos on Mac allow you to store full-resolution photos and videos on iCloud instead of an internal hard drive, which makes storage more efficient. Although you do not want to store all files and documents on iCloud, you can free up space on your hard drive while keeping your photos safe.

Your photos will remain on your Mac's hard drive until they begin to fill, where photos and videos (from the oldest) will be removed from the Mac and stored only on iCloud.

Photos and videos frequently take up a lot of space. You may find that your iCloud storage space is not enough to store an entire library in iCloud. If you run out of time, you can upgrade your iCloud storage to a larger program.

  ∘ How to use photo and video storage on Mac

iCloud Photo Library

iCloud Photo Library is part of the Apple iCloud service that helps you back up, sync, and share photos and videos. This is all the data you require to know.

Cloud Photo Library allows you to access all your photos and videos on all devices at any time. It's an optional part of the Apple iCloud app, and you can enable it at any time and use the latest iCloud device to upload all new photos and videos from the "Photos" app to your iPhone, iPad, or Mac.

Take video on iPhone, take a photo with an iPad, import a photo from DSLR to the Mac version of the picture - if the iCloud Photo Library is enabled, all of this will be uploaded to the iCloud repository, where possible !).

Cloud Photo Library can have many features: photo backup, sync services, archive tools, photo sharing sites, and more. It can help you to make the little management of photos and videos a thing of the past. Here's how to do it right!

What is Cloud Photo Library?

iCloud Photo Library is an optional feature of the Apple iCloud service, which can automatically back up and sync any photos and videos you take on iCloud. It works with iPhone, iPad, and Mac photos, and also provides synchronization services for devices like Apple TV. When iCloud Photo Library is enabled, it will use the iCloud storage space to upload all the photos and videos you take, screenshot, save or import to any iOS or Mac device.

Over the years, many people have asked me if I should use this service: Is it safe? is it safe Is the cost of the iCloud program worth it? This is thin.

> ➤ Cloud Photo Library: Should you use it?
> ➤ Cloud Photo Library and My Photo Stream: What's the difference?
> ➤ Cloud Photo Library and security: What you need to know!
> ➤ What photo library storage program should you get?

How to set up iCloud Photo Library

iCloud Photo Library will store photos, videos, GIFs, screenshots, and more, or better yet, after enabling you, you can use "Optimize Storage" to send files to iCloud instantly and protect them from taking up your iPhone's storage space.

This is a way to set up iCloud Photo Library on iPhone, iPad, Mac, PC, and Apple TV to backup photos and videos, expand storage to the device, and share photos with friends and family.

- ➤ How to set up Cloud Photo Library on iPhone and iPad.
- ➤ How to set up Cloud Photo Library on Mac.
- ➤ How to fixed up iCloud Photo Archive on Windows 10
- ➤ How to fixed up iCloud Photo Archive on Apple TV

How to use and manage the Cloud Photo Library

Once you subscribe to the Apple iCloud app and enable the iCloud Photo Library, you can access the photo and video library on any device — even if they can't store these photos locally. The "Photos" app for iPhone, iPad, and Mac (as well as the "iCloud Photos" app on PC) can easily view photos you've taken on your current device or saved them in the gallery; and works with your iCloud library Sync library, where you can view content stored on any device.

We provide a guide on how to view photos stored on iCloud next to local photos, edit and share them, view them online or offline, keep your photos private, and how to prevent iCloud Photo Library from taking all your photos. storage space.

- ➤ How to use iCloud Photo Library on iPhone or iPad
- ➤ How to use iCloud Photo Library on Mac
- ➤ How to use iCloud Photo Library on Apple TV
- ➤ How to custom iCloud Photo Archive on iCloud.com

- ➢ How to view iCloud photo library images when you are offline
- ➢ How to separate private photos from Cloud Photo Library
- ➢ How to use the storage space on an iPhone or iPad
- ➢ How to use storage space on Mac

How to set up and use iCloud photo sharing

Apple's iCloud app includes iCloud photo sharing, allowing you to share photos and videos with friends, family, and colleagues on your iPhone, iPad, Mac, PC, or Apple TV. While technically speaking, iCloud photo sharing is part of the iCloud Photo Library, iCloud photo sharing is not within the scope of the app: you do not need to use iCloud Photo Library to share photos, and shared albums are not counted in the archive for iCloud.

Most importantly, creating a shared album is easier and safer than posting photos on Facebook or Instagram: your photos and videos remain private between your groups, and you can delete the album at any time. If you want to attract more people, you can create a public Cloud.com website to host photos of anyone and provide links to view them.

- ➢ iCloud Photo Sharing: A Final Guide
- ➢ How to set up photo sharing via iCloud
- ➢ How to view and create shared albums
- ➢ How to like, comment, and add subscribers to shared albums
- ➢ How to share photos with family sharing with iCloud

How to Save and Resolve Cloud Photo Library

- ➢ How to Save Your iCloud Photo Library
- ➢ Troubleshooting Cloud Photo Library
- ➢ How to Save iCloud Photo Library to the iPhone or iPad mobile data system

Everything you need to know about Cloud Music Library

Apple offers two music subscription services that can be used with iCloud Music Library: iTunes Match and Apple Music

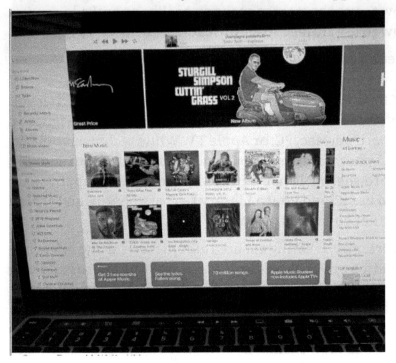

Cloud Music Library is an Apple service used to store your online music library with "same" tracks and songs included in the iTunes Store (or by directly uploading tracks if there are no similarities). You can then stream and download them (without DRM) until they reach other registered devices of your own.

If you sign up for Apple Music, you'll get the iCloud Music Library as part of a $ 9.99 monthly subscription; If not, you can sign up for the Apple iTunes Match service and pay $ 24.99 a year to keep the iTunes library on an iCloud song (up to 100,000 songs)).

Looking for a new music listening gadget? Check out our recommendations for the best iPhone!

How iCloud Music Library works

Both Apple Music and the independent iTunes Match service include something called iCloud Music Library. Here's what you need to know.

What is Cloud Music Library?

This is what Apple calls all the music stored on iCloud.

Pause, is it saved? Does it count my final cost of iCloud?

No. Sign up for Apple Music or iTunes Match, you can save up to 100,000 songs; does not count depending on your iCloud storage costs.

Can it be used with Apple Music and iTunes Match?

Yes, the Apple Music subscription service and iTunes Match standalone options are available. Cloud Music Library lets you upload or "move" your library to a DRM-free iTunes Store identifier.

If you have an Apple Music account, you can use the iCloud Music Library and subscribe to music; If you have a separate iTunes Match subscription, you can only access the iCloud Music Library.

➢ Apple Music vs iTunes Cup tie: What's the modification?
➢ If I have Apple Music, do I still want iTunes Match?
➢ iTunes Game: The Ultimate Guide

How to deal with matching, storing.

When you sign up for Apple Music or the independent iTunes Match service, Apple scans the iTunes Music Library to view and see if your tracks are also listed in the iTunes Store.

To save space and download time, any library tracks are also provided in the iTunes Music Store catalog, and will "match" the catalog version. This means that if you play a track on your iPhone or another Mac, you will get a version of the iTunes Music

Store (for those who want to know, it is a 256kbps DRM-free AAC file) instead of the original file. Apple uses audio and video metadata fingers to match your songs to the iTunes Store. Incomplete, and you may have problems with live or unusual tracks such as the studio version — but for most users, you should be able to use the app without any problems.

Any song other than the iTunes catalog will be uploaded to iCloud in its original format, unless the audio track quality is too low (less than 92kbps), too long (over two hours), too large (over 200MB), or you do not have the rights of Google Play (for example, songs from other iTunes users accounts, you do not have a username and password to unlock).

If you have a song included in ALAC, WAV, or AIFF in your library, it may be transferred to the AAC 256 Kbps file when you upload to iCloud; The original file in the iTunes library cannot be changed.

Once your songs have been uploaded, they will be stored or synced to your iCloud music library; any device you have (up to 10) can stream or download songs to it.

Note: Currently, you need an iTunes library containing 100,000 songs or less for the iCloud Music Library to work properly. If there are too many songs, please follow the steps below to create a second iTunes library.

What do I get from the Cloud Music Library?

Lots of stuff! Mac Library can be found on any other device (up to 10).

If you are a subscriber to Apple Music, it also allows you to add songs and playlists from the subscription catalog to your music library; then, you can save these tracks for offline playback.

Do I need to back up before enabling iCloud Music Library?

Of course, it is. exactly. Cloud Music Library can provide you with copies of songs in the cloud, but it has never been a support service. So, please heed our warning: before opening the iCloud Music Library, make sure you have a complete copy of all your local music on your computer (or external hard drive).

How to Save iTunes Library

If you have enabled it and do not have all the local music on one computer, please don't panic: make sure your music is shown as "matching" or "uploaded" instead of "Apple Music", and download all non-tracks on your big Mac.

Why should I not use Cloud Music Library?

If you do not have a backup of your Mac data, or have too many tracks with conflicting metadata, and are concerned that iCloud will be corrupted or do not want to store songs offline in Apple Music, you will need to turn off the iCloud music database and leave.

Can I use Apple Music without the iCloud Music Library?

You bet you can even use the iCloud Music Library on some devices, but not on others. More details here:

➢ How to use Apple Music without the Cloud Music Library

I opened the iCloud Music Library and swallowed my library / destroyed everything-ah! Help?!

She took a deep breath. Do you have a backup? If so, turn off the iCloud Music Library on your Mac, and restore your library to a file.

If there is no backup, you can try other actions, from chatting with Apple support to reset iCloud Music Library. If you have a problem and do not have a backup, we recommend that you review the troubleshooting guide below:

➢ **Problem Solving Apple Music: A Final Guide**

What the Cloud Music Library can and cannot do

Now that we have explained what the iCloud Music Library is, the following is a brief introduction to what it can and cannot do.

With the Cloud Music Library, you can.

- Broadcast your Mac media library to up to ten different devices (including 5 Macs or Windows PCs)
- Delete the same audio tracks you have on your Mac, and download them again for a higher version of 256kbps DRM in the iTunes Store (useful if your audio tracks are low).

you will not know

- Manually sync music from iTunes to your iPhone: now everything is done wirelessly.
- Use iCloud Music Library for family sharing: Each Apple ID (and its iCloud Music Library is independent; however, you can download all purchased items from iTunes.
- Align or upload over 100,000 tracks from your purchased music library in the iTunes Store: If you still want to use the iCloud music library, but there are too

many tracks, please create a second iTunes library.

- ◦ Apply to all countries/regions: This is a list of countries/ regions for Apple Music Library supported by Apple.

Note: If you only use the independent iTunes Match service for $ 24.99 per year, the iCloud Music Library will not allow you to access the music in the Apple Music catalog: you need to sign up for Apple Music for this.

How to support iCloud Music Archive on your computer

If you have an Apple Music account:

> ➢ **How to enable or disable Cloud Music Library**

If you are interested in subscribing to and using the Cloud Music Library with iTunes Match:

1. If you're signed in to your iTunes account, please open the "Music" app on your Mac (or open the iTunes app on Windows) and navigate to the "Account" menu.
2. Click Exit.
3. Select the iTunes Store on the left.
4. Scroll down and select "iTunes Match" under "Features".

5. Choose "Subscriptions" for $ 24.99 per year.
6. Enter your Apple ID and password.
7. After the registration is complete, select "Use iCloud Music Library".
8. Click Install this computer to upload and synchronize the computer library with the iCloud library. (This step can happen automatically, so if you don't see it, don't panic.)

Adding a Mac or Windows PC is similar to the first registration process for iTunes Match users. If you accidentally create separate collections on your personal computer and computer, this is also a great way to integrate your music library - if the Cloud Music Library is enabled on both computers, you can download all the songs on a second PC or Mac To your main computer.

1. On the second Mac, open iTunes and navigate to the "Account" menu.
2. Click Exit.
3. Click the "Match" tab displayed in iTunes (or go to "Account"> "iTunes Match").
4. Choose "Subscriptions" for $ 24.99 per year.
5. Enter your Apple ID and password. (You may need to enter it twice.)
6. Choose to use iCloud Music Library to use it on this computer.
7. iTunes will remind you to sign up for iTunes Match and ask if you want to use it on this computer. Click Install this computer to connect a computer library to the iTunes Match and iCloud music library.

Note: If you did not choose to set up Apple Pay when you start your MacBook Air, you can set it up later in the "Wallet and Apple Pay" window of "System Preferences". Manage your Apple Card and other payment cards here add or remove cards and update contact details.

Learn more. See the articles that support Apple's "Setting up Apple Pay", "How to Use Apple Pay" and "Managing Apple Pay used cards".

Use AirPrint on Mac

You can use AirPrint wireless to print at:

- Printers are powered by AirPrint on Wi-Fi networks
- Network printer or shared printer for another Mac over Wi-Fi network
- The printer is connected to the USB port of the AirPort base station

Print and print for AirPrint. When you print from the app, click on the "Printer" menu from the "Print" dialog box, then select the printer from the "Nearby Printers" list.

Can't find the printer you want? Make sure you connect it to the same Wi-Fi network as the MacBook Air. If you are connected but still do not see it, try adding it: open System Preferences, click Printers & Scanners and click the Apply button. (You may need to use a USB cable and adapter (if necessary, temporarily connect the printer to the MacBook Air).)

Learn more. See wireless printing from Mac to AirPrint printer in macOS Guide.

For a list of printers that support AirPrint and other supported printers, see the Apple support article "About AirPrint".

Use AirPlay for Mac

Use AirPlay screen view to show everything on the MacBook Air on the big screen. To mimic a MacBook Air screen on a TV screen or use HDTV as a second display, connect the HDTV to an Apple TV and make sure Apple TV and MacBook Air are on a similar Wi-Fi system. You can also play online videos directly on HDTV without displaying desktop content, which is great for you if you want to play movies but doesn't work in private.

Use a screen display to mimic the desktop. Click the "Control Center" icon in the menu bar, click "Screen mirroring", and then click on "Apple TV". When AirPlay is enabled, the icon becomes blue.

Note: If your Mac supports AirPlay screen view, when Apple TV and Mac are on the same network, you will see an AirPlay status icon in the Mac menu bar. See Use AirPlay play video or mimic the device screen.

In some cases, you can use the AirPlay display even if the MacBook Air and Apple TV are not on the same Wi-Fi network (also known as the peer-to-peer AirPlay network). To use Peer-to-Peer AirPlay, you need an Apple TV (third generation rev A, model A1469 or higher) with Apple TV software 7.0 or higher.

Play web videos without showing off the desktop. When you find a web video with an AirPlay icon, click on the icon, then select your Apple TV.

Tip: If the image does not fit your HDTV screen when viewing the screen, please adjust the desktop size to get the best picture. Click the AirPlay icon in the video and select the option under "Match Desktop Size".

Apple TV is sold individually at Apple.com or your native Apple Store.

Learn more. To learn further about AirPlay, see "Use AirPlay to stream at ease from Mac to HDTV" in the macOS user guide. To learn more about using the second display on the MacBook Air, see Using the external display on the MacBook Air. To resolve the issue, please refer to the Apple support article If AirPlay or Screen Mirroring is not available on your device.

Use the Apple Watch to unlock Mac and enable tasks

If you're wearing your Apple Watch, you can use it to automatically turn on your MacBook Air and enable authentication functions, such as password entry, unlock notes and preferences, and authorize installation without typing a password. These features use robust encryption functions to provide secure communication between Apple Watch and MacBook Air.

Use automatic opening and approval of Apple Watch functionality:

- Use the same Apple ID to sign in on Mac and Apple Watch.
- Make sure the Apple Watch is turned on and uses watchOS 3 or higher to unlock Mac automatically; watchOS 6 or higher is required to approve the authentication request.
- Turn on two-factor authentication (see below).

Set up two-factor verification in your Apple ID. To turn on dual authentication, go to Apple menu> System Preferences> Apple ID> Password and Security, and select Set up two-factor authentication. Please see the Apple support article Two-factor authentication for Apple ID.

Make sure "Disable auto-login" is also selected. (If you are using FileVault, you will not see this option, but you can still use the "Auto Unlock" and "Approve with Apple Watch" features. For details on FileVault, see File Vault Encryption for macOS User Guide Mac details.)

Set default unlock. Sign in to all devices with the same Apple ID, then open "System Preferences" on the MacBook Air. If your Apple Guard has watchOS 6 connected, click "Security and Privacy", then click "General" and select "Use Apple Watch to open apps and Mac." If your Apple Watch has watchOS 3 to watchOS 5 installed, please select "Allow Apple Watch to unlock Mac". Unless you have watchOS 6 or higher, you cannot authorize authentication activities.

Note: These functions will only work if your Apple Watch has passed password verification. Every time you install your Apple Watch, you need to authorize it, so there is no need to take any additional steps after entering the password.

Skip login. Install the guaranteed Apple Watch on your wrist, go to the sleeping MacBook Air, then lift the protective cover or press the key to open the MacBook Air-Apple Watch to unlock it, so you can work normally.

Approved using Apple Watch. When you are told the password, double-click the separate button on the Apple Watch to confirm the password on the Mac. You can view passwords in Safari, allow app installation, unlock locked notes, etc. (WatchOS 6 required).

Apps

Installed Apps with Mac

MacBook Air comes with a series of excellent applications to meet your daily tasks, such as surfing the Internet, sending emails and messages, and setting up calendars. There are also apps like Photos, Apple Music, Apple Podcast, Apple TV app, pages, numbers, and Keynote, so you can create and produce from scratch. The following sections describe the applications installed with the MacBook Air.

Note: Some MacOS programs are not available in all regions or languages.

Get more apps. Click the App Store icon in Dock to get the app for all the things you want to do. To learn more, see the App Store.

Get help with any app. When using the app, tap the "Help" menu (located in the menu bar at the top of the screen). Please refer to the macOS User Guide.

the app store

Search the App Store to find and download apps, and get the latest updates for apps.

Get a perfect application. Do you know exactly what you want? Enter the name of the application in the search field and press Return. The apps you download from the App Store will automatically appear on the launchpad. If you click on the "Categories" tab in the sidebar, you can also find new Safari extensions that can add value to your personal browsing experience.

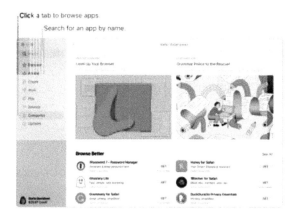

Note: Apple Arcade is not accessible in all realms or regions.

Ask Siri. It says: "Look for children's apps."

You only need an Apple ID. To download the free app, please sign in with your Apple ID - select "Store"> "Log In", or click "Log In" at the bottom of the sidebar. If you do not have an Apple ID, click "Sign in" and then click "Construct an Apple ID". If you have an Apple ID but have forgotten your password, click "Forgot Apple ID or password?". Replace. You must also set up an account with detailed purchase information to purchase paid apps.

Use iPhone and iPad apps on Mac. Many iPhone and iPad apps can now run on MacBook Air. All existing apps that you previously purchased with your iPhone or iPad will be displayed on your Mac. Search apps in the App Store to see if they're available on Mac.

play games. Click the "Arcade" tab to learn how to sign up for the Apple Arcade, find games to play, find games that your Game Center likes your friends, check out the progress of success, etc. See "Subscribe to Apple Arcade" in the App Store on Mac, Apple Arcade, and Play games on Mac.

Get the latest updates. If you see the badge in the App Store icon in Dock, an update is available. Click the icon to open the App Store, then click Update in the sidebar.

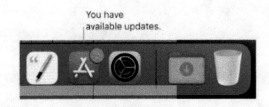

You have available updates.

Books

Use Apple Books to read and edit your library and audiobooks, and buy new books on your Mac.

Note: Apple Books are not available in all countries or regions.

A bookshelf on Mac. Browse or search all items in the library, or click "Bookstore" in the sidebar and select a category to find new books and other publications. To purchase goods, just sign in with your Apple ID (select Store> Login).

Ask Siri. Say something like: "Look at Jane Austen's book."

View your books.   Type what you're looking for.

Never lose your position or tag. As long as you sign in with the same Apple ID, you can automatically use purchased books, collections, key content, notes, bookmarks, and the current page you are reading on Mac, iOS, and iPadOS devices.

Find a way back. You can quickly go to the specified page. Click the arrow next to the bookmark button to view your bookmark list

Tip: Switch to the "Night" theme for easy reading in low light conditions. Select "View"> "Theme" and "Night", or click the "Appearance" button and then click the black circle. Not all books support the theme of the night.

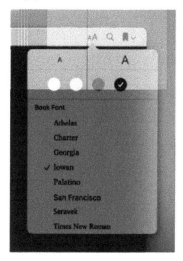

Calendar

Never miss an appointment with a calendar. Keep track of busy schedules by creating multiple calendars and managing them all in the middle.

Create an event. Click the Apply button to enter a new event, or double-click anywhere per day. To invite someone, double-click an event, click the "Add guests" section and type in an email address. The calendar notifies you when invited to respond.

Show the calendar list.   Create a new event.   Change the calendar view.

Tip: When you add a place to an event, "Calendar" will show you a map, estimated travel time and travel time, and weather forecasts. Force force on any event in the calendar to see more details.

View all of your calendars — or just a few. Click the Calendar button to see a list of all calendars. Click what you want to see in the window.

A calendar for all aspects of life. Create different calendars (for example, home, work, and school calendars), each with its color. Select "File"> "New Calendar" to create a calendar, then hold the Control key and click on each calendar to select a new color.

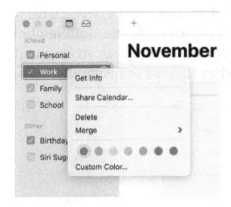

Share between your devices and others. After logging in to iCloud, your calendar will be kept up to date on all Mac, iOS devices, iPadOS, and Apple Watches devices that sign in with the same Apple ID. You can share calendars with other iCloud users.

Find my

Use "I Found" to find your friends, family, and Apple devices - all in the same app.

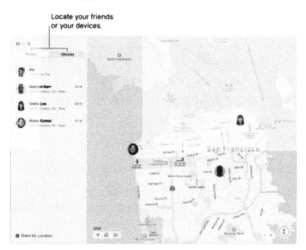

Note: Not all regions or languages offer the "I found" feature.

Share location with friends. In the "People" list, click "Share my location" to tell friends and family your location. You can share places for an hour, a day, or indefinitely, and stop sharing anytime, anywhere. You can also ask to follow friends so you can see their location on the map and learn their location step by step.

Set location alarms. When you arrive or leave a place, automatically send a notification to your friends. Set notifications when friends leave and arrive. When your friend creates notifications about your location, you can view all the notifications by clicking on one "Me" in the "People" list and then scrolling to "Notifications about you".

Protect lost equipment. Use "Find Me" to locate and protect a lost Mac, iPhone, iPad, iPod touch, Apple Watch, or AirPods. Click the device in the device list to find it on the map. Click the Details icon to play audio on the device to help you find it, mark the device as missing so that other people can access your personal information, and you can wipe the device remotely.

Find devices even when they are offline. When my device is not connected to Wi-Fi or a mobile network, "Find Me" will use the Bluetooth signals of other nearby Apple devices to locate your device. These symbols are anonymous and encrypted, helping to locate lost devices without compromising privacy.

Find devices for family members. If you are in the "Family Sharing" group and your family members are sharing their location with you, you can use "Find Me" to help find family member devices.

Garage Band

GarageBand is an app for creating, recording, and sharing music. It has your recording studio at home and everything you need to learn to play a musical instrument, write music, or record songs.

Create a new project. You can start from the song template, select the speed, keys, and other options, then click "Record" and start playing. Create your song — for example, use different tracks and loops. Click Quick Help and hover the mouse cursor over objects to understand what they are and how they work.

Show Smart Controls.

View Editors.

Tracks area

View Apple Loops.

Open the Note Pad.

Rhythm. You can use Drummer Loops to quickly add drums to your project. Click "Loop Browser", then drag "Drummer Loop" to the empty section of the "Songs" area. You can customize the drummer loop to suit your song using a simple set of controls.

Record your voice. Select "Songs"> "New Track", then select the microphone under "Audio". Click the triangle next to "Details" to set the installation, extraction, and monitoring options, and then click "Create". Click the "Record" button to start recording, or click the "Play" button to stop recording.

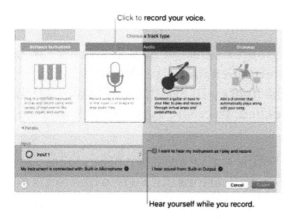

Click to record your voice.

Hear yourself while you record.

Home

With the Home app, you can easily and securely control all Home-
eKit accessories from your Mac.

Controlling accessory. Attachments are displayed as tiles with
symbols in the home app. Click the accessory button to control
the light and turn off the lights, lock or open doors, view live cameras, etc. You can also adjust the light intensity or temperature of
the thermostat. The new overview of the Home app shows a summary of attachments that require your attention or need to share
important status changes.

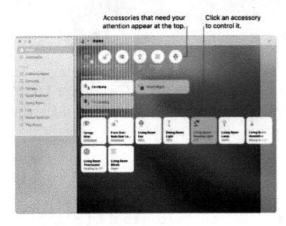

Shared access. You can share the house with your family or guests
so they can use the "Home" app to control accessories on their
Apple devices.

Create a group. Create a group so that your accessories can be
used with a single command. For example, make a good nightlife,
when you go at night, all the lights will be off, the shadows will be
off, and the doors will be locked. To create a group, click, and then
click Apply Status.

HomeKit security video. Define active areas within camera view
to capture video or receive notifications only when motion is de-
tected in these areas. In addition to personal, animal, and vehicle
information, face recognition can also allow security cameras

and doorkeepers to see the people you mark in the "Photos" or "Home" app as recent visitors. (HomeKit Secure Video requires a Family Center and a compatible iCloud program. For more information, see the Home User Guide

Changing lighting. Set up your smart bulb to automatically adjust its color temperature throughout the day to increase comfort and productivity. Get up with warm colors, concentrate and remind during the day with cool colors, and turn off the blue light at night to reduce stress. (Adjustable lighting requires a home hub. For more information, see Setting up a router on a Mac for use with the home in the Home User Guide.)

iMovie

With iMovie, you can convert home videos into beautiful movies and Hollywood styles, which can be shared with just a few clicks.

Import video. Import videos from existing media files to your iPhone, iPad, or iPod touch, camera, or Mac. The movie makes you a new library and events.

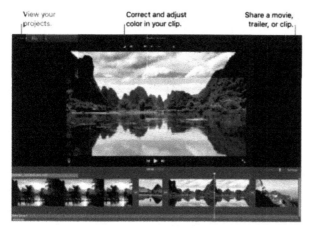

Use the built-in camera to record video. Use the FaceTime HD camera on your Mac to record video and add it to your project. Select the event in the sidebar, click "Import" in the toolbar, select FaceTime HD Camera, and click the "Record" button to start and stop recording.

Create a trailer with Hollywood style. Make smart trailers with vivid graphics and flying songs. Just add photos and video clips and customize subtitles. First, click the "New" button, click "Trailer", select a template from the "Trailer" window, and then click "Create". Insert characters and subtitles on the "Framework" tab, then add your photos and videos to the "Summary" tab.

Click Play to preview the trailer.

Tip: Using portable devices to shoot videos may produce unstable effects, but you can stabilize the video to make the play smoother. Select a clip from the timeline, click the "Stable" button, and then click "Stable Shaking Video".

keynote

Use Keynote to create professional presentations. Start with one of the more than 30 pre-made themes and make your own by adding text, new items, and changing the color scheme.

Visual organization. Use the left navigator on the left to quickly add, rearrange or delete slides. Click the slide to view it in the main window, drag the slider to change its layout, or select a slide and press the Delete button to remove it.

Exercise makes perfect. To practice the presentation, select Play> Practice Slides. You will see all the slides and notes, and there is a watch to keep you on track.

See how you're doing on time.

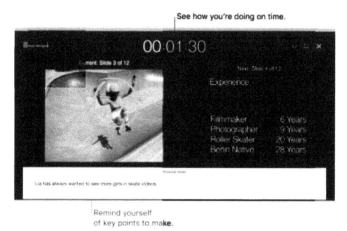

Remind yourself
of key points to make.

Share your presentation. If your administrator wants to view your presentation, or you want to share the presentation with others on the conference call, please select "Share"> "Send Copy" to send a copy by mail, message, AirDrop, or through social media.

Attract them. Attract their attention by animating objects on the slide Select the item, click "Animation" in the toolbar, click "Working" in the sidebar, and then click "Apply Effect".

Tip: You can add a video to your presentation. Click the location you want, then click the "Media" button in the toolbar. Click on the movie, then find the movie you want and drag it to the slideshow.

Mail

Email lets you manage all your email accounts in one application. It can be used with popular email services such as iCloud, Gmail, Yahoo Mail, and AOL Mail.

One-stop email. Tired of accessing multiple websites to check your email account? Set up email with all accounts so you can view all your mail in one place. Select "Mail> Add Account".

Ask Siri. Say something like this: "Are there any new emails from Laura today?"

Get the right message. Type in the search field to see suggestions for messages similar to your query.

Focus on the essentials. View only the messages you want to see in your inbox. You can block messages from specific senders in the following ways: move them directly to "Trash", mute the active email thread, and then unsubscribe directly from the Email list.

Enter events and contacts directly from Mail. When you receive a message containing an email address or a new event, simply click "Add" to add it to "Contacts" or "Calendar". Force the address to see a preview of the location, which you can open on the map.

Personalize any message. Just click to add an emoji or image. Select a photo from the photo library, or take a photo on your iPhone or iPad. You can also add drawings to iPhone or iPad. To learn more about importing

images and graphics from other devices, see Continuity Camera on Mac and Continuity Sketch and Continuity Markup on Mac.

View fullscreen. When you use "Mail" in full screen, a new mail window will automatically open in "Split View" on the right, so you can easily quote other mail in your inbox when you compose an email. Please see the Apple support article Using two Mac apps next to Split View.

Split the "Mail" window on the screen and display two separate messages.

Don't miss the email. Check the "Mail" icon in the Dock to see the digit of unread emails. When a new email is received, a notification will also be displayed at the top right of the screen so you can preview the incoming message. (Don't need notifications? To turn off notifications, open "System Preferences" and click "Notifications.")

Map

Use maps or satellite imagery to get directions and view places. Find tips on the best in town in Apple's preferred guide. Force push into place to place a pushpin on it.

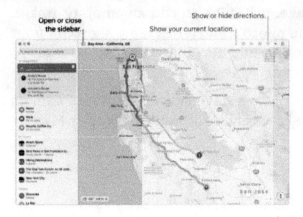

Open or close the sidebar.

Show or hide directions.

Show your current location.

Explore new places with your guide. To help you find the best places to eat, shop, and explore the world, the map offers selected guides provided by trusted brands and partners. You can keep these guidelines and update them as new locations are added.

Create your guide. You can create your guide to your favorite places and share them with friends and family. To create a guide, hover over the "My Guide" in the sidebar, click the "Add" icon on the right, then hold down the Ctrl key and click on the new guide to see the options menu.

3D test. Click on the "Looking Around Binoculars" icon to browse the selected city in 3D, so you can navigate through the streets in a more immersive experience.

View internal maps of major locations. Find a way out of certain airports and supermarkets. Just zoom in to see restaurants near your door, find toilets, arrange a meeting place with friends at the mall, and more.

Ask Siri. Say something like this: "Get coffee near me."

Take public transportation to get there. The map provides details of the public transportation of a particular city. Click the destination bar in the sidebar, and then click the navigation icon to get the suggested route and estimated travel time.

Scheduling an electric car ride becomes easier. Install your electric car on your iPhone, and Google Maps will show you the location of the charging station on the route and consider the charging time when the ETA counts.

Plan your bike route. The map gives you the information you need to plan your bike ride, such as altitude, traffic conditions, and whether there are small slopes. After planning your trip, you can send it to your iPhone.

Get real-time ETA updates. When friends and family members share their estimated time of arrival with you, a map can show you where they are on the route.

Warning: For important information about roaming and to avoid potential interference, please see the Important Security Information for Mac.

Tip: To view the flow, click the "View" menu in the menu bar, then select "Show flow".

Message content

With messages, you can stay connected easily no matter what

device you're using. With iMessage, you can send unlimited messages to anyone on a Mac, iOS device, iPadOS device, or Apple Watch. Connect with one or more people and manage group discussions with online responses and comments. See Apple's support article "About Messages and SMS / MMS".

Sign in and post. Sign in with Apple ID to exchange unlimited messages, including text, photos, real-time photos, videos, etc. Anybody with a Mac, iPhone, iPad, iPod touch, or Apple Watch. For setup details, see the Apple Support Messaging article on Mac.

Tip: If your iPhone (using iOS 8.1 or later) is signed in with the same Apple ID as a message, you can send and receive SMS or MMS messages on your Mac. On your iPhone, go to "Settings"> "Messages", click "SMS Forwarding", and then click the name of your Mac to open "SMS Forwarding". On a Mac, if you don't use the authenticity of two Apple ID items, you'll see a usage code. Enter the code on the iPhone and tap "Allow".

Keep your favorite conversations high. Drag your favorite conversation to the top and paste it at the top of the message list. New messages, minimal rewind, and typing directions will be displayed on top of the modified chat. When there are unread messages in a group discussion, new participants will appear next to the scheduled conversation.

Management team dialogue. By setting a photo, Memoji, or emoji as a group photo, the group can be easily identified. In a group chat, you can direct a message to someone by typing that person's name or using the @ sign, and you can answer questions by adding comments as a queue at the beginning of the conversation. When the conversation is very active, you can hide the warning of that conversation. To set a group photo and view chat management options, select a conversation from the list and click the "Details" button in the top right corner of the "Messages" window. To be notified when you receive your notification, open "Messaging Preferences", click "General", and select the "Let me know when my name is mentioned" box.

Make the message interesting. Reply to messages using Tapbacks, trending GIFs, or special effects (such as hitting confetti, balloons, etc.) to make the conversation more lively. To install a tapback, click and hold the message, then select Tapback. To insert a GIF or special effect, click the "Applications" button, select "#Image" or "Message Effect", and then click the image you want to use. Also pay attention to Digital Touch, invisible ink, and handwritten messages that your friends send to you from your iPhone, iPad, or Apple Watch.

Add a photo, sticker, video, or effect.

- Photos
- Memoji Stickers
- #images
- Message Effects

Send Memoji stickers. The post will automatically generate a sticker packet based on your Memoji characters. To add Memoji stickers to a conversation, click the "Applications" button, then "Memoji Stickers", and then click the sticker that best expresses your feelings.

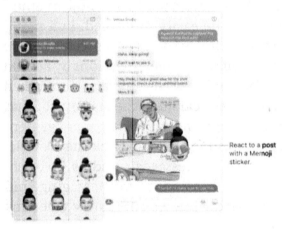

React to a **post** with a Me**moji** sticker.

Create your own Memoji. Design your custom meme Memoji - choose skin and spots, hairstyle and skin tone, facial features, and more. To use personalized Memoji as a picture message, go to Message> Preferences. Click Edit name and photo sharing, click Continue, and then click Customize. Click the "New Memoji" button, and then click on each function to create a look. When you're done, click "Finish" to add the Memoji to your sticker collection. To add more Memoji to your collection, please open a conversation, click the Apps button, Memo Stickers, the new Memoji button, and create a fun design.

Post files, photos, or videos. You can easily share files by dragging them to "Messages". Or quickly find and send photos and videos from your photo library. In the chat, click the "Applications" button, then click on "Photos", then click Insert Image. Enter keywords (for example, person name, date, or location) in the search field to help you find specific images.

When the text is inadequate. Switch off messages and record audio or video calls with messages If your chat partner has Face-Time, click

"Details" button in the message window, then click the "Call" button or the "Video" button to start the FaceTime audio or video chat.

Screenshot of the "Messages" window and its "Contact" menu.

Share your screen. You and your friends can share screens, even open folders, create texts, and copy files by dragging them to the desktop on a shared screen. Click the Details button, then click the share screen button.

Music

The Apple Music app lets you easily start up and enjoy purchased iTunes Store purchases, songs and albums in your file and the Apple Music catalog (you can pin your ears back to millions of wanted songs) Click to watch the next song, previously played track and lyrics. Buy the music you want in the iTunes Store.

It's on your bookshelf. You can easily view and play items purchased in the iTunes Store, items added to the Apple Music catalog, and music in your database. Filter content by recently added artists, albums, or songs.

Browse the best Apple Music. Click "Browse" in the sidebar to view new music and special versions of Apple Music, a music streaming service that requires a monthly fee. Stream and download over 50 million songs without ads, then select from multiple playlists to get the best mix at any given time.

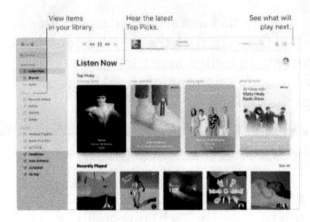

sing together. Click the "English" button on the toolbar to display a panel with the characters of the current song (if available).

Listen. Click "Radio" in the sidebar to listen to Apple Music 1 live streaming or listen to any episode in the Apple Music series. Explore channels for almost all genres of music.

Ask Siri. It says: "Play Apple Music 1."

Easily sync. Sync your music content directly to the Apple Music app. When the device is connected, you will see it in the Finder sidebar. Just drag the content you need to the device. You can also back up and restore devices to Finder.

Shop in the iTunes Store. If you want to have music, click the iTunes Store on the sidebar. (If you do not see the store in the sidebar, select "Music"> "Favorites", click "General", then click on "Show iTunes Store.")

Tip: When the screen space is very valuable, please switch to MiniPlayer to open a small floating window, you can drag it to the desired location to listen and control the music while performing other tasks on your Mac. To unlock MiniPlayer, select "Window"> "MiniPlayer".

News

Apple News is a stand-alone newsletter with the information provided by editors selected and personalized. You can save the article for future reading, and read it offline or on other devices. Apple News + allows you to read hundreds of magazines, popular newspapers, and leading digital publishers in one month.

Note: Apple News and Apple News + are not available in all countries or regions.

Customize your feed. Follow your favorite channels and topics to view them in the "Today" feed and sidebar. Enter the media or articles in the search field and click the "Apply" button to track.

Tip: If you are reading an article and want to save it for later use, select "File"> "Save Story". To view the article later, click "Saved News" near the top of the sidebar. If you sign in with the same Apple ID, you can access articles from any device.

Notes

Notes are not just text. Write down quick ideas, or add a checklist, photos, weblinks, etc. Shared folders allow you to share an entire notes folder with a group, and everyone can participate.

Ask Siri. Say something like: "Create a new note."

Choose Gallery view.   **Create a checklist.**   **Share folders of notes.**

Tip: When you sign in with your Apple ID and turn on iCloud notes, your notes are kept up to date on all devices, so you can create a to-do list on your Mac, and use your iPhone on the go.

Customize your toolbar. Right-click on any toolbar to open a custom window. Drag your favorite items to the toolbar to suit you.

View list. Click the "List" button to enter the interactive list on the note, and the note will automatically send selected items at the bottom of the list. Select "Format"> "More"> "Uncheck all" to uncheck all items in the list and start reusing your weekly shopping list.

Include photos, videos, etc. Drag photos, videos, PDFs, or other documents from the desktop. Select "Window"> "Image Browser" to add items from the photo library to notes.

Set the table. Click the table button to insert a table into your notes. You can even copy tables from web pages or other applications and paste them into your notes.

Lock the note. You can set a secret code to lock notes that you don't want others to see. To set a password, select Notes> Preferences, and then click Set Password. To lock a note, select a note, then select File> Lock Note.

Number

Use numbers to create engaging and powerful spreadsheets on Mac. More than 30 templates designed by Apple allow you to create budgets, invoices, group rosters, and more. Prices can open and export Microsoft Excel spreadsheets.

Start with a template — and add what you need. Select a text sample from the template, and then type new text. To add an image, drag the image file from Mac to a proxy image.

Sort sheets. Use multiple worksheets or tabs to display different views of your details. For example, use a piece of paper to make a budget, another piece of paper on forms, and the third piece of paper to get notes. Click the Add button to add a new worksheet. Drag the tabs left or right to rearrange the worksheet.

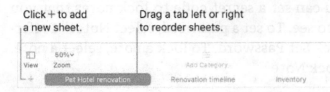

Click + to add a new sheet.

Drag a tab left or right to reorder sheets.

The formula is very simple. For built-in help with over 250 powerful functions, simply type an equal sign (=) in the cell and you will see a list of all the functions and their descriptions in the sidebar. Start typing formulas for quick suggestions.

Tip: For a quick calculation of a series of values, select the range of cells that contain these values. At the bottom of the window, you'll see the total, average, minimum, quantity, and calculation of the selected values. Click the menu button in the lower right corner to see more options.

Pages

Use the Pages app to create great documents and books on Mac. Open and edit Microsoft Word files, and track changes made by you and others.

it looks great! Pages contain professional, ready-to-use books, media releases, reports, resumes, and other templates to easily start your project.

Add charts, movies, and more.

Open or close the Format sidebar.

All your formatting tools are in one place. Click the "Format" button in the toolbar to open the "Format" tester. Select an item in the text, and its formatting options will appear.

Make a note around the drawing. When you insert an image into text, the text will automatically flow around the image. You can edit the text wrap in the "Format" sidebar.

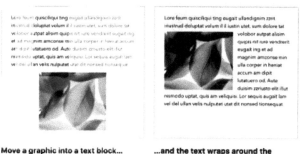

Move a graphic into a text block...   ...and the text wraps around the graphic automatically.

Start on Mac, start on iPad. If you sign in with the same Apple ID, you can keep documents on all devices up to date. So, you can start composing an image on one device and continue working where you left off on another device.

Tip: Enable tracking of changes to see changes made to a document by you and others. Everyone's settings and comments are colored, so you can see who made each change. Select Edit> Track Changes to display the Tracking Toolbar.

Picture

Use "Photos" and "iCloud Photos" to edit, edit and share your photos and videos, and keep your photo library up-to-date on all devices. "Photos" show your best photos, and with powerful search options, you can easily find and enjoy your favorite photos. Easy-to-use editing tools allow you to customize photos and videos like a professional.

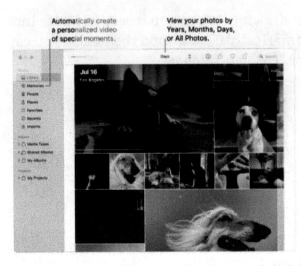

All photos on all your devices. With iCloud Photos, you can browse, search, and share all photos and videos on all devices signed in with the same Apple ID. When you take a photo on your iPhone, the photo will be automatically synced to other devices. Additionally, when editing photos, this setting will be displayed on all devices. First, open "System Favorites", click "Apple ID", click "iCloud", and then select "Photos". To learn more, see the Apple support article "Setting and using iCloud Photos."

Plan as an expert. Create beautiful photos and videos with easy-to-use editing tools. Use the edit button above the image or video to enhance it with a single click. To use more powerful editing tools, click "Edit" and use "Smart Slider" to get technical results. You can add filters, rotate, increase exposure, and crop photos and videos.

Change view. "Photos" show the best photos in your library, hide duplicates, receipts, and screenshots. Viewing photos of a specific date, month or year is easier than ever, or click on "All Photos" to quickly view your entire collection.

Remember the good times. When you scroll, real-time photos and videos start playing, and your photo library comes alive. Click "Memories" in the sidebar to enable "Photos" to find the best photos and videos and create memorable movies (including music, themes, and transition effects), that you can create and share. You can check the memory on all other devices that use iCloud photos.

Get the perfect lens. Photos can point to objects, groups, and people in your photos and videos. Search for images based on the content of the image, the date is taken, the person by name, the additional title, and the location (if provided).

People and places. "Photos" understand your photos (including people and what happened to them) and highlight important moments such as birthdays, reminders, and visits. Click the "Favorites" button on someone else's photo to make that person a favorite, and that person will always appear at the top of the album. Use the "Location" album to view all photos with location data on an interactive map. Zoom in on a map to show more photos of specific places.

Tip: You can add location details to any photo. When viewing an image, click the "Info" button, then click "Provide Location" and begin typing. Select a location from the list, or type a location, then press Return.

Use real-time photos to be creative. When using "Live Photo", use the "Loop" effect to continue wrapping the action, or use "Bounce" to play animation back and forth. To look like a high-end DSLR camera, use "Long Exposure" to blur the "Live Photo" movement and turn ordinary waterfalls or streams into works of art.

Podcast

Use Apple Podcasts to browse, subscribe and listen to your favorite Podcasts on your Mac.

Start listening now. One store to set up new episodes of the podcasts you subscribe to, and personalized recommendations for podcasts you might be interested in. After you sign in with your Apple ID or start listening to other devices, all podcasts you're listening to will be saved to "Listen Now".

Save the episode to your media library. To save one episode in your media library, click the Insert button. To accompany new episodes of the entire podcast, click "Subscribe". To download the podcast for offline listening, click the "Download" button.

Discover new podcasts. Find selected feeds for new podcasts in "Browse" or see which shows are best in "Top Charts." If you see your favorite show, please subscribe to the podcast or add an episode to the library for later use.

Search for a landlord or visitor. When searching for a specific topic or person, you can view the shows they hosted, guest shows, and the results of the places mentioned or discussed.

Tip: You can use AirPlay to play podcasts, music, or radio with external speakers. Click the "Control Center" icon in the menu bar, click "Screen mirroring", and select the available speaker.

Reminders

Reminders make it easier than ever to keep track of all your activities. Create and edit menu lists, projects at work, or anything else you want to follow. You can also choose when and where the reminders are. Get teams to assign shared project tasks.

Keep a log of this in a smart list. The Smart list automatically organizes your upcoming reminders in four categories. Select Today to see all your reminders scheduled for today, as well as any expired reminders. Select Schedule to see your reminders of dates and times with a single timeline view. Select Flag to see the reminders you marked as important. Select All to see all your notices in one place.

Use wise suggestions. Reminders automatically suggest dates, times, and locations of reminders based on the same reminders you created in the past.

Give the burden. Give reminders to the people you share the list with, so they can get notified. Divide the tasks and make sure everyone knows where you are responsible. To share a list, select File> Share List.

Organize by sub-activities and groups. To convert a reminder into a sub-task, press Command-], or drag it above another reminder. A parent's reminder is bold, and a little work has been put under it. You can drop or expand your subtitle activities to keep your viewing less crowded.

To group reminders, select File> New Group. Name the group whatever you would like to do. Add more lists by dragging them to a group, or remove them by dragging them out.

Receive reminder suggestions in the Mail. When you write to someone in Email, Siri sees potential reminders and makes suggestions for you to create them.

Install the reminder immediately. Use natural language to quickly add a reminder. For example, write "Take Amy to the ball every Wednesday at 5 PM" to create a recurring reminder of that day and time.

Safari

Safari is the fastest and most effective way to browse the web on a Mac. A customized homepage can contain your favorite background and features you want to view, such as "favorites", frequently visited websites, Siri suggestions, your reading list, iCloud tags, and privacy reports. The label now contains an easy-to-identify website icon and provides a preview when you move the cursor over the label. With support, you can also get the faster translation of websites into other languages.

Note: Not all regions or languages offer translation skills.

Start searching. Start typing in the name or address of the website — Safari will show you similar websites and suggested websites. Or select the items you like or frequently visited on the Safari home page.

Customize your first Safari page. Your homepage can display "favorites", "read lists" items, privacy reports, etc. You can import a special image to use as a background image, or you can select one of the given backgrounds. Click the "Customize Safari" icon in the lower-right corner of the home page to set options for the first page.

Get an extension. Extensions add features to Safari to customize your browsing experience. You can find shortcuts and useful information, display news headlines, and instantly share content on your favorite apps and services. The new extension section in the App Store has Safari extensions, which include outstanding editing and popular charts to help you find and download useful items. See App App. After receiving the extension, please open it in Safari preferences. Select the Extensions tab, then click the check box to open the extension.

View multiple web pages in one window. Click the "Add" button to the right of the tab, or press Command-T to open a new tab and enter an address. To make it easier to use a web page, please drag its tab to the left to adjust it, and save it to the tab bar.

Take a quick look at the contents of the label. An icon on the label (a logo or logo associated with a website) allows you to see a web page at a glance. Move the cursor over the tab to see web content previews.

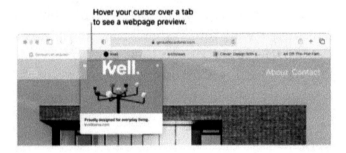

Hover your cursor over a tab to see a webpage preview.

Use strong passwords. When you sign up for a new account on the web, Safari will create and fill you with a strong password. If you choose to use a strong password, the password will be stored on your iCloud key and will be automatically filled in on all devices you sign in with the same Apple ID. Safari securely scans your passwords, identifies all stored passwords involved in possible data breaches, and makes it easy to upgrade to a "Sign in with Apple" account (if available). (See "Log in with Apple on Mac" in the macOS Operator Guide.)

Browse the web safely and privately. Safari will alert you if the website you are visiting is unsafe or attempts to trick you into sharing your personal information. By identifying and deleting data left by the tracker, it can automatically protect you from site tracking. Safari will ask for your permission before allowing social networks to view your activities on third-party websites. Safari protects web tracking by making it harder for your Mac to identify differently.

View Privacy Report. You can click the "Privacy Report" button on the Safari Toolbar to view site tracking programs where Safari blocks each website and better understand how that website handles your privacy. Click the "Full Report" button to view the privacy statement, which contains detailed information about the website activity tracker.

Translate web (beta) pages. You can instantly translate the entire web page into Safari. If you encounter a Safari translation page, you will see a translation button website address field. Click to translate between the following languages: English, Spanish, Simplified Chinese, French, German, Russian and Brazilian Portuguese. The button changes color to a blue translation icon to display when a web page is translated.

Tip: On a web page, you are forced to click on a word to view its meaning, if available, click on the Wikipedia article. Try forcing text by clicking on other apps like Messages or Mail for more details.

Open image-in-image. When playing a video, click and hold the "Audio" button on the label, then select "Insert image-image" from the menu below. Your video appears in a floating window, and you can drag and drop a window so you can watch it while performing other tasks on your Mac. You can also set the auto play s submenu option here. To mute the video, click the "Audio" button.

Stock

The Stocks app is the best way to track a market on a Mac. View prices in the list of custom watches, click on stocks to see detailed details and interactive charts and learn about driving trends with news from Apple News.

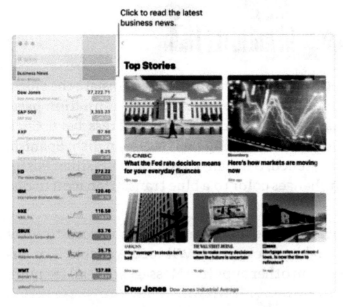

Note: Apple News news and popular news are available in the United States, Canada, the United Kingdom, and Australia. Yahoo has provided news reports from other countries and regions.

Customize your watch list. To add stock to the watch list, enter the company name or stock code in the "Search" field, hold the Control key and click on the stock in search results, then click

"Add to Watch List". To remove stock, hold down the control button and click the stock icon, then click "Remove from watch list". You can also hold the Control key and click to open stock on a new tab or window.

Check for market changes. When viewing the watch list, click the green or red button under each price to rotate between price changes, percentage changes, and market value. The watch list includes color-coded sparklines that track results throughout the day.

Read articles about the companies you follow. Click on the watch list to view interactive charts and other details, and read the latest news about the company.

understand deeply. Want to see what the flea market was doing last week, last month, or last year? Click the button at the top of the chart to change the timeframe and view the price with your preferred view.

Your watch list for all devices. When signing in with the same Apple ID, keep a watch list compatible with all devices.

Tip: Click on "Business News" at the top of the watch list to view a collection of timely business articles selected by Apple News.

TV

Watch all movies and TV shows in the Apple TV app. Buy or rent movies and TV shows, subscribe to channels, and stop and watch from any device.

Start watching now. In "Watch Now", browse the selected feed options based on the channels you've subscribed to and the movies or TV shows you watch.

Keep watching Next. In "Next", you'll find movies or TV shows you watch, as well as movies and TV shows added to the line. To add a new movie or TV program to "Next", click the "Add to" button.

Find out more about movies, TV shows, and kids. If you want to find specific content, please click on the movie, TV, or children's tab in the menu bar, and browse by type.

Buy, rent or subscribe. After you find a movie or TV program you want to watch, you can choose to buy or rent it. Your subscription channels are available on all devices, and up to six family members can be used for family sharing.

Choose something from your library. Click on the media library to view all the movies and TV shows you have purchased or downloaded by genre. To start watching, just click on a movie or TV game.

Voice invitation

Voice invitations make recording personal reminders, class talks, and even interviews or song ideas easier than ever. With iCloud, you can directly access iPhone-recorded voice memos on Mac-Book Air.

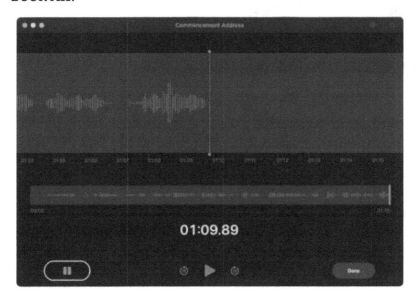

Record from MacBook Air. Click the "Record" button to start recording, then click "Finish" to pause. You can rename the record to make it easier to see. Click the default name and enter a new name. To play the recording, click the "Play" button.

Your voice memo on all devices. When you sign in with the same Apple ID, a voice memo is available on all devices. You can access the recordings made via iPhone or iPad directly from your Mac.

Arrange folders. Create folders to help you keep your voice memo organized. To add a folder, click the sidebar switch, then click the new folder key at the end of the sidebar. Enter a folder name and click "Save". To add a recording to a folder, hold the Option key while dragging the recording to a folder.

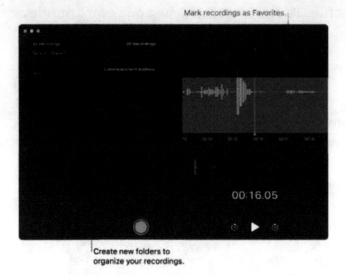

Mark recordings as Favorites.

00:16.05

Create new folders to
organize your recordings.

Mark recording as a favorite. Select a video, then click the "Favorites" button on the toolbar, so you can quickly find the video later. Click the sidebar to view all the favorites.

Improve the recording effect. Improve the sound quality of voice memos by reducing background sound and room restorations. Click "Edit" at the top of the "Voice Memo" window, then click the "Play" button, then click the "Upgrade" button.

Find answers

macOS User Guide

The macOS User Guide provides more details on how to use the MacBook Air.

Get help. Click the Finder icon in the Dock, then click the "Help" menu in the menu bar, then select MacOS Help to open the macOS User Guide. Or type a question or word in the search field and select a topic from the results list.

Check the title. To find articles in the MacOS user guide, you can browse or search. To browse, click "Table of Contents" to view the list of topics, and then click a title to read it. Or type what you want in the search field to get the exact answer.

Click > to view more topics. Click a topic to read it.

Learn about new features. Click the "Help" menu and select "See what's new in macOS" to learn more about the latest macOS features.

Tip: If you do not remember the location of the menu item in the app, please search for "Help". Place the cursor on the result and the arrow will show you the command.

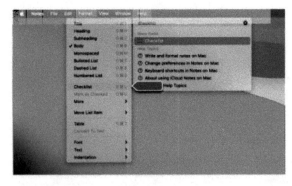

Frequently asked questions about Mac

How can you get MacBook Air support? Go to MacBook Air support.

I'm new to Mac. Are there any tips for PC users? Yes, that's right! See the Apple Mac support article for Windows switch tips. Check out the basics of Mac for a quick tour. You may be interested in keyboard shortcuts on your Mac.

How to take a screenshot on a Mac? Press Command-Shift-3 to take a full screenshot. Press Command-Shift-4 to take a screenshot of the selected location on the screen. To learn more, see

Taking a screenshot on a Mac.

What is my serial number? Select the "Apple" menu> "About this Mac". The serial number is the last item on the list. You can also find the serial number at the bottom of the MacBook Air.

Ask Siri. Say something like: "What is the serial number of my computer?"

How do I know which MacBook Air model I have? See Apple's support article "Identify MacBook Air Model". You can also select the Apple menu> About this device to view model details.

How can you get MacBook Air documents? For the Essentials guide, select the Apple menu> "About this Mac", click the "Support" tab, and then click on "User Manual." On the "Support" tab, you can also click "MacOS Help" to open the app's user guide. For older Mac models, please refer to product browsing manuals.

How can you get help to apply? When using the app, click the "Help" menu in the menu bar at the top of the screen.

What is the security information for the MacBook Air? See important Mac security details.

How can you get technical specifications? Go to the specifications of MacBook Air technical, or select Apple menu> About this Mac, then click the up button.

Ask Siri. Ask Siri for details about the Mac. Say this:
- "How fast is my Mac?"
- "How much money does my Mac have?"
- "How much free universe is at hand on my Mac?"
- "How many universes do I leave in an iCloud room?"

How can you check if there is a problem with the disk? Use Disk Utility. Please refer to the "Disk Utility User Guide" in Disk Utility on Mac to configure storage devices.

What should I do before selling or trading on a Mac? Back up data, and restore Mac to factory settings. Before you sell, offer, or trade your Mac, see what you do.

How do you reinstall macOS? Use macOS to restore. See how to reinstall macOS in macOS recovery.

Note: Starting with macOS Big Sur, Time Machine backups do not include program files. See Back up and Restore a Mac.

Keyboard shortcuts for Mac

You can press a combination of keys to perform tasks that you would normally use a trackpad, mouse, or other devices to perform on your MacBook Air. The following is a list of the most commonly used keyboard shortcuts.

Shortcut	meaning
Commandment-**X** it to	Cut out the selected item and copy the clipboard.
Commandment-**C**	Copy the selected item to the paste board.
Commandment-**V** or application.	Paste the clipboard contents into the current document
Command-**Z** to reset.	Undo the last command. Press Command-Shift-Z
Commandment-**A**	Select all items.
Command-**F** ment.	Open a search window or search for items in this docu-
Command-**G**	Find the next match for the item you want. Press Com-

mand-Shift-G to get the previous position.

Command-**H**	Hide previous app window. Press Command-Option-H to view previous other apps.
Command-**M**	Minimize the front Dock window. Press Command-Option-M to minimize all windows of the previous application.
Command-**N**	Open a new document or window.
Command-**O**	Open the nominated item or open a dialog box to select a file to open.
Command-**P**	Print the current document.
Command-**S**	Keep the current document.
Command-**W**	Close the front window. Press Command-Option-W to close all application windows.
Command-**Q**	Exit the current app.
Command-**Option-Esc**	Select an application to force quit.
Command-**Tab**	Switch to the next application use between open ap-

plications.

Command-**Shift-5** also	Turn on screenshot usage. You can

use the following
shortcuts to take

screenshots:

- Press Command-Shift-3 to take a full screenshot.
- Press Command-Shift-4 to take a screenshot of the selected location on the screen.

If you are switching from PC to Mac, please see the Apple support Mac Tips article for Windows Switcher for a list of Mac keyboard shortcuts and differences between Mac and Windows keyboards, and what's the name on Mac? For more keyboard shortcuts, check out Apple Keyboard shortcuts.

Safety features on MacBook Air

MacBook Air provides security features to protect computer content and to protect unauthorized software programs during download:

- Safe storage: The MacBook Air storage drive is encrypted with a key committed to its hardware to withdraw advanced security. In the event of a disastrous failure, data recovery may not be unlikely, so you need to back up your files to an external source. See Apple's support commentary "About Encrypted Storage on a New Mac". You can set Time Machine or other gridlock programs to back up your computer regularly. See the macOS User Guide to use Time Machine to back up files, and Apple support Article Use Time Machine to back up your Mac.

- Safe boot and boot utility safe: Safe boot supports automatic unlock. It is designed to ensure that the software downloaded to the computer is not first approved by Apple. See Apple's support article "About Safe Boot.

If the MacBook Air fails to run due to unreliable discovery, it will open up from secure partitions and automatically fix the problem if possible. To learn more about "Starting Security Utility" or to learn how to set up some options (for example, boot from an external device), see the Apple Support Article "About Starting a Security Service."

- System integrity: The Apple M1 chip is designed to ensure that the first-time macOS software version is approved by Apple and continues behind the scenes to protect the established macOS authorization during operation. This makes it very difficult for malware or malicious websites to take advantage of your Mac.
- Data protection: In addition to the default encryption drive for MacBook Air, third-party application developers can use file-level encryption to better protect sensitive data without affecting system performance.

Save space on MacBook Air

With Backup Setup, you can automatically free up space on your MacBook Air by providing files on demand. Your original files will be stored on iCloud and IMAP email or Exchange server, so you can download them at any time. Some tools can identify and delete large files.

Configure storage. To view storage recommendations, go to Apple menu> About this Mac, click Storage, and then click Manage. Depending on how you set up your Mac, you'll see various suggestions. If you have enough storage space on your Mac, you will see a warning with a link in the store window.

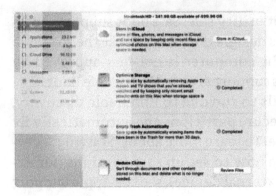

Set options to:

Save to iCloud: Save all files, photos, and messages to iCloud and save space on your Mac.

- Desktop and Documents: Save all files in the "Desktop and Documents" folder on Cloud Drive. When storage space is required, Cloud Drive will store newly opened files on Mac and provide older files as needed.
- Photos: Save photos and videos to iCloud photos. When storage space is required, iCloud photos use advanced types of photos and videos on a Mac and provide real where on-demand.
- Email: Save all emails and attachments to iCloud. When storage space is required, iCloud will store the latest attachments to the Mac and provide the original files as needed.

Even if your files are stored in the cloud, you can access them by storing them in the appropriate location on your MacBook Air. See Access iCloud content on Mac.

Customize storage: Save space on your Mac by storing movies and TV shows in the Apple TV app. You can choose to automatically delete movies or TV shows after watching MacBook Air. You can download them again at any time.

Automatically empty the trash: Automatically wipe the contents of the trash for more than 30 days.

Reduce confusion: easily identify large files and delete unwanted files. To browse large files, click the sidebar - books, documents, iCloud drive, email, messages, create music, photos, dump paper, etc.

To help you save working space, macOS also:

Prevent yourself from downloading the same file from Safari twice

Remember to uninstall the software once you have finished installing the new app

Clear logs and storage that can be safely removed when storage is inadequate

Learn more. Please refer to Optimizing Storage Space on Mac in the System Information User Guide.

Mac resources, services, and support

You can find more information about MacBook Air in system reports, Apple diagnoses, and online resources.

System report. For details about MacBook Air, use the program reports. It shows the hardware and software installed, the serial number and operating system type, the amount of memory installed, and so on. To open the program report, select Apple menu> About this Mac, and then click System Message.

Apple Diagnosis. You can use Apple Diagnostics to help determine if there is a problem with one of your computer objects (such as memory or processor). Apple Diagnostics can help you determine the cause of a potential hardware problem and provide a first step in trying to resolve the problem. If you need more help, Apple Diagnostics can also help you contact AppleCare support.

Before using Apple Diagnostics, disconnect all external devices, such as hard drives or external displays. Make sure the MacBook Air is connected to the Internet.

To start Apple Diagnostics on your MacBook Air, restart your computer and hold the power button for 10 seconds to turn on "Startup Options", then press and hold Command-D to enter Diagnostics mode.

When prompted, select your local language. Press Return or click the right arrow button. The basic test of Apple Diagnostics takes a few minutes to complete. If a problem is found, the description of the problem and other instructions will be displayed. If you need to contact AppleCare, please write down all the reference codes before Apple Diagnostics is out.

Online resources. For online service information and support information, go to "Welcome to Apple Support". You can read about Apple products, browse online brochures, check for software updates, contact other Apple users, and get Apple's services, support and advice. For more information on MacBook Air, see MacBook Air support.

AppleCare support. If you need help, and AppleCare representative can help you install and open the app and resolve the issue. Call your nearest help center (free for the first 90 days). When making a call, please set a purchase date with the MacBook Air serial number.

For a complete list of support phone numbers, please visit the Apple website for assistance and service. Phone numbers can change at any time, and country and home values can be used.

Your 90-day free support starts from the date of purchase.

Take a screenshot on a Mac

Browse through the "Screenshot" menu to find all the controls needed to take screenshots and screen videos. You can also take a voice during screen recording. Customized workflow allows you to take photos and videos on-screen and easily share, edit or save them.

Access screen control. Press Command-Shift-5. You can capture the entire screen, the selected window, or part of the window. You can record the entire screen or selected parts of the screen.

Use the icons at the bottom of the screen to take selected shots, the "screen selection screenshot" icon, the screen recorder, the "screen recorder" icon, and more. Click on options to change your storage location, set the timer before shooting, set the microphone and audio options, or display directions. Click Take or Record to take a screenshot or video.

After taking a screenshot or video, an icon will appear in the corner of the screen. Drag the icon to the document or folder and swipe right to save it immediately, or click Edit or Share.

Note: You can also open the "Screenshot" app from the "Other" folder in the launchpad, or go to the "Applications"> "Applications" folder in Finder.

Tag your screenshot. Click on the screenshot icon to use the marking tool and explain. You can also click the "Share" icon to send a marked screen to colleagues or friends directly from the screen itself. See marking files on Mac in macOS user directory.

Tips and Tricks

Install iPhone and iPad apps

The M1 SoC uses the same construction and A-series chips on the iPhone and iPad. This means you can finally run iPhone and iPad apps locally on the M1 MacBook Air and Pro.

Go to the Mac App Store, search for an app (such as Overcast or Facebook), and switch to the "iPhone and iPad apps" tab. After that, you can select the iPhone / iPad app, install it like any other app on your Mac, and open it with a Spotlight search or with the touchpad.

Catch; the developer should make iPhone and iPad app versions available on Mac, so you may not see popular apps (like Instagram or Gmail) in the Mac App Store.

You can also show a list of purchased/installed apps on iPhone and iPad. Just select your profile from the bottom left corner of the Mac App Store and switch to the "iPhone and iPad Apps" tab to access it. After that, start installing the required applications.

View touch options

All the iPhone and iPad apps you can install on your Mac are designed for use on the touch screen your M1 MacBook isn't. As a solution, Apple used something called a "touch substitute". It is a combination of trackpad touch and keyboard buttons that can be used to communicate with these apps. You can call the preset commands by selecting the "Touch Overlay" option in the menu bar of the app-based touch.

Adjust the background light of the keyboard

If you want to adjust the brightness of the M1 MacBook Air keyboard, you will no longer see related access controls. Instead, you should use the Control Center (this is one of the great new features on macOS Big Sur).

Just tap the "Control Center" sign at the top right of the menu bar. After that, select the keyboard light and move the left or right lighting slide to increase or decrease the brightness.

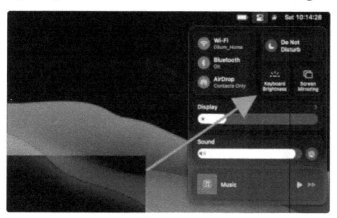

Insert icons in the menu bar

As you may have noticed, the Control Center brings together almost all of the previously existing icons in the menu bar. This keeps things organized, but as you have to dive deeper into the control center, accessing the Wi-Fi or Bluetooth menus also becomes more difficult.

Thankfully, you don't have to endure it, just drag the icon out of the "Control Center" and return it to the menu bar. This also applies to controls such as "Brightness of the keyboard" and "Display".

Appointment, recognition, and non-interference

Apple may have discarded the keyboard back control from the M1 MacBook Air task line, but similar buttons point to other useful macOS functions. You can now use "Dictation" and "Do Not Disturb" by pressing F5 and F6 respectively. Besides, the F4 key (which had previously launched launchpad) can now deliver Spotlight search.

Put It to sleep

The M1 chip is a beast. Close and open the lid, and your MacBook Air or Pro should wake up quickly, like the iPhone and iPad. This gives you enough reason to put it to sleep to save battery life.

Change accent marks to multicolor

The macOS Big Sur also comes with a "multicolor" option located to the left of the "Accent" ribbon under "Preferences System"> "General". Select it, each program can have its color scheme.

Disable wallpaper color

If you do not like the color of the wallpaper on older MacBooks, you no longer need to be patient. Go to System Preferences> General> and uncheck the "Enable wallpaper color setting for Windows" option.

Manage notifications immediately

macOS Big Sur comes with an advanced notification center. Notifications are now packed with the app, making it easier to manage. Best of all, and you can manage notifications directly.

Right, click on a notification stack or specific application. Then, select "Send in peace" to send notifications silently to the notification center, or click "Close" to disable future alerts for this application.

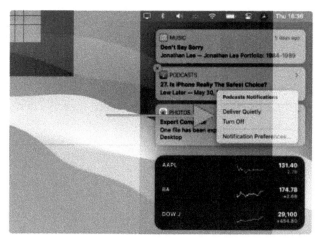

Check the M1 compatibility of the application

Not all apps you install on the M1 MacBook Air or Pro are designed for Apple Silicon. However, the M1 chip is so fast that it can easily run Intel-coded programs with the Rosetta 2 Translation Environment integrated. But also, apps designed for these two chips (Apple likes to call them "universal") should quickly launch on your M1 MacBook Air and have the best performance.

To check if a particular application has traditional M1 chip support, start by going to the "Applications" folder in Finder. After that, right-click on the app and select the "Get Info" context menu option. If you see "Application (General)" next to "Category", the application is configured for chip M1. If you use Application (Intel) instead, the system will work in the same way as Rosetta 2 translated.

Keep your application up to date

If you have unsolicited applications on your Mac, please be sure to update them regularly, as they may provide native Apple Silicon support in advance. Go to the Mac App Store and switch to the "Updates" tab to install the latest updates. If you downloaded an app outside the Mac App Store, try finding the update option within the app.

Manage and edit widgets

macOS Big Sur comes with iPhone-like widgets, and you can access them via the notification center on your M1 MacBook Air or Pro. Although you can't drag them to the desktop or place them on top of each other, you can add a widget library to add and remove widgets, and easily choose between different sizes. To do this, use the "Edit Widget" option at the bottom of the notifications center.

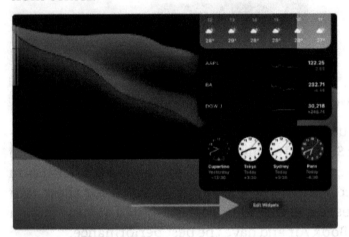

Additionally, you can right-click on any widget and switch between sizes without dragging it down to the widget library. For some widgets, you have a right-click menu option for "Edit widget", allowing you to change the widget function. For example, you can use it to change the time zone in the "World Clock" widget.

Install third-party widgets

You can also load third-party app loads with widget support by briefly jumping into the App Store. If you do not like to hunt near the App Store, please use this story chosen by Apple.

Start using Safari again

On macOS Big Sur, Safari has achieved significant performance improvements, making it 50% faster than Chrome. The situation is much better on the M1 MacBook, where you can open multiple tabs without stopping work. If you are using a performance test like Chrome, please consider giving Safari another chance.

Watch YouTube in 4K

Safari also supports YouTube in 4K. As we all know, the M1 chip on the MacBook is so fast that it can handle multiple video streaming at 2160p without effort.

Customize Safari

Finally, Safari comes with a custom "start" page that allows you to easily add your personality. Just select the "Custom" icon in the lower right corner of the screen, and you can quickly enable or disable "Favorites", "frequent access", "privacy reports" and other components. Additionally, you can add a domain to the "home page" - select one of the built-in domains, or upload your image.

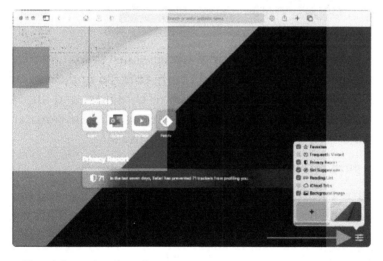

Edit videos in the photo app

Video editing on M1 MacBook Air or Pro is best suited for iMovie or Final Cut Pro. However, if you are fast, the "Photos" app on macOS Big Sur should be able to help you. You now have access to the entire set of editing options that were previously reserved for photos only. Switch to "Edit" mode while watching the video to try it out.

Update the M1 MacBook Airor Pro

The M1 MacBook Air and M1 MacBook Pro are amazing devices. However, they are relatively new, and you will inevitably experience various errors, malfunctions, and stability problems as you continue to use them. Therefore, be sure to get the latest software updates as soon as they become available (which usually resolves known issues).

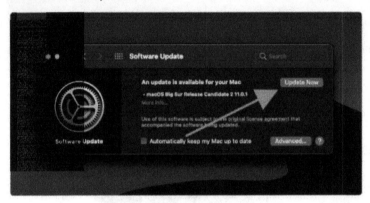

macOS Big Sur also makes additional updates faster and less intrusive, so you have no reason to add them, toff. To update your Mac, go to "System Preferences"> "Software Updates" and apply all updates (if any). If you want your Mac to update itself, you can check the box next to "Automatically update my Mac".

Show battery percentage

Speaking of battery life, by default, the M1 MacBook Air and Pro will not display the battery percentage in the menu bar. This is a design decision made by Apple on macOS Big Sur, and it usually works on all MacBooks. If you want to check the battery percentage, you should now bring up the "Battery Status" menu by selecting the battery indicator.

However, you can return the battery percentage indicator to the menu bar if needed. To do this, open the Apple menu, select System Preferences, and then click the Dock & Menu Bar icon. After that, switch to the "Battery" sidebar and check the box next to "Show percentage

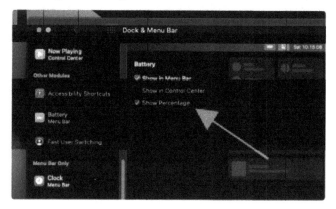

Check battery usage statistics

macOS Big Sur also introduced a new battery panel, which shows battery usage statistics, such as the iPhone and iPad. You can do this by selecting the "Battery" icon in the "System Favorites" window. This may be helpful if the battery in your M1 MacBook starts to discharge immediately and you do not know why. The battery panel also contains energy savings from the very beginning of macOS.

Set the highlight color

If you are tired of seeing the same blue buttons and symbols on the M1 MacBook Air or Pro, try enhancing the color by changing the highlighting color. Navigate to the "System Favorites" window, select "General", and select your favorite color from the "Emphasis" tab. You should immediately notice changes in all areas.